Good People

Good People

David Lindsay-Abaire

THEATRE COMMUNICATIONS GROUP
NEW YORK
2011

Good People is published by Theatre Communications Group, Inc.,
520 Eighth Avenue, 24th Floor, New York, NY 10018-4156

This publication is made possible in part with public funds from the New York State Council on the Arts, a State Agency.

TCG books are exclusively distributed to the book trade by Consortium Book Sales and Distribution.

Library of Congress Cataloging-in-Publication Data
Lindsay-Abaire, David.
Good people / David Lindsay-Abaire.—1st ed.
p. cm.
ISBN 978-1-55936-393-8
I. Title.
PS3562.I511925G66   2011
812'.54—dc22   2011013517

Book design and composition by Lisa Govan
Cover design by Spotco
Front cover: Tate Donovan and Frances McDormand; photo by Alison Rosa

First Edition, May 2011
Second Printing, March 2012

Good People

Production History

Good People received its world premiere by Manhattan Theatre Club (Lynne Meadow, Artistic Director; Barry Grove, Executive Producer) on Broadway at the Samuel J. Friedman Theatre, on March 3, 2011. *Good People* was commissioned by the Bank of America New American Play Program. The production was directed by Daniel Sullivan. The set design was by John Lee Beatty, the costume design was by David Zinn, the lighting design was by Pat Collins and the sound design was by Jill BC DuBoff. The dialect coach was Charlotte Fleck, the production stage manager was Roy Harris and the stage manager was Denise Yaney. The cast was:

MARGARET	Frances McDormand
STEVIE	Patrick Carroll
DOTTIE	Estelle Parsons
JEAN	Becky Ann Baker
MIKE	Tate Donovan
KATE	Renée Elise Goldsberry

CHARACTERS

MARGARET: white, about fifty
STEVIE: white, late twenties
DOTTIE: white, mid-sixties
JEAN: white, about fifty
MIKE: white, about fifty
KATE: African American, early thirties
VARIOUS OFFSTAGE VOICES: probably prerecorded

PLACE

The play is set in South Boston's Lower End, and in Chestnut Hill, Massachusetts.

NOTES

A slash (/) in the dialogue indicates the start of the next spoken line.

The name "Margie" is pronounced with a hard "g" in the middle, not a "j."

Act One

———

Scene 1

South Boston, Massachusetts. The alley behind the Dollar Store. There's a dumpster back there, a rusty chair, and a door labeled DOLLAR STORE— DELIVERIES ONLY. The back door opens and Margaret, about fifty, comes out with Stevie, her manager, late twenties. Stevie carries a folder.

MARGARET

Did she ever tell you the turkey story? Up at Flanagan's?

STEVIE

No.

MARGARET

When I worked up there, and she came in? She never told you that turkey story?

STEVIE

I don't think so.

MARGARET

She was pregnant with you. No, Jimmy actually—she was pregnant with Jimmy—because it was near Christmas, and your father was locked up in Walpole again, so she didn't have any money for anything.

STEVIE

(Offers her the rusty chair) You wanna sit down?

MARGARET

She had nothing. Except Saint Vincent de Paul's. Thank god for them. They used to give out toys at Christmas to the ones who couldn't afford it.

STEVIE

Margaret, listen for a / second—

MARGARET

(But she keeps going) I don't think they did Christmas dinners though. And your grandmother had passed by then, so there was no dinner to go to. So your mother comes into Flanagan's, and she's out to here. *(Indicates belly)* When's Jimmy's birthday?

STEVIE

January.

MARGARET

Right, so she's out to here, and in this *big* coat. Remember that blue coat she always wore?

STEVIE

Yeah.

MARGARET

And she's walking up and down the aisles, slipping things in the pockets—potatoes, and cans of cranberry sauce, cookies, because

6

you guys gotta eat, right? So she comes waddling up to my register. And I'm like, "Hey Suzie, how are the kids?" And she doesn't wanna talk obviously, she's just trying to push through the line: "Oh, they're good, I was just looking for something, but you don't have it, so I'm gonna try someplace else." And then the turkey falls out of her coat. It hits the floor right between her legs. A turkey. Boom.

And I swear to god, she didn't miss a beat. She looks up, real mad, and yells, "Who threw that bird at me?!"

(Really laughing now) Oh, we died. Everybody there. Ya had to laugh. "Who threw that bird at me?!" She was a funny sonofabitch. Pardon my French.

STEVIE

Look, Margaret—

MARGARET

God, she was funny. I think about her all the time. Your mother was a good lady. It's a lesson though. You're lucky you don't smoke. Too young, your mother.

STEVIE

Can we do this?

MARGARET

(Beat) Sure. *(Moves to the chair)* You gotta make them give you a real office, Stevie. Because these alley conferences? No way to run a business. It smells back here.

STEVIE

I know you don't wanna talk about why I brought / you out here—

MARGARET

No, I know. I was late, I'm sorry.

STEVIE

It's just, the district manager / comes in—

MARGARET

I know. It was my Joycey again. You know I can't leave her alone
when she gets outta sorts. And I pay Dottie Gillis a little bit to
keep an eye on her, but Dot's not the most reliable.

STEVIE

Right, but the district manager comes down on *me* about it.

MARGARET

No, I know, that guy's an ass—pardon my French.

STEVIE

Maybe, but he's also my boss. And he looks over those punch
cards.

MARGARET

Okay.

STEVIE

No, not okay. You're late every day. Twenty, thirty minutes.
Yesterday it was almost an hour.

MARGARET

It's not every day.

STEVIE

Pretty much it is, and that reflects badly on *me*. He wants to know
why I can't keep my employees in line.

MARGARET

You have to explain about Joyce. She's in a program, thank god,
but that's only so many hours a week. I can't / always—

8

STEVIE

I explained it to him, but there's only so much / I can—

MARGARET

It's not just me, Stevie. Karen calls in sick every couple days.

STEVIE

Yeah, well, I'm talking to Karen next.

MARGARET

Well, while you've got her out here, you should ask her why she tells everyone you're gay.

STEVIE

(Beat) What?

MARGARET

She says you're gay.

STEVIE

(More bemused than offended) I'm not gay.

MARGARET

I know.

STEVIE

So why does she say that?

MARGARET

Because you go to bingo.

STEVIE

That makes me gay?

MARGARET

I'm just tellin' ya what Karen says to people. You go to bingo a lot. More than I do. More than Karen does.

STEVIE

I like bingo.

MARGARET

Obviously.

STEVIE

Plenty of men go to bingo.

MARGARET

I wouldn't say plenty, but yeah.

STEVIE

Freddy Gleason goes to bingo.

MARGARET

Yeah.

STEVIE

Frank Moore.

MARGARET

Yeah. A few old-timers, but yeah, that's what I've been telling her.

STEVIE

Okay, it doesn't matter.

MARGARET

Are you gonna bring it up with her though?

STEVIE

No, I'm going to say to her exactly what I'm saying to you. The district manager came / in—

MARGARET

She's late a lot more than I am.

STEVIE

Okay.

MARGARET

And she says you're gay.

STEVIE

Margaret—

MARGARET

I know you're not gay, and I tell her that, because you're dating what's her name. I don't know if that's supposed to be a secret, or whatever, but everybody knows that. Not Karen, obviously, but everybody knows that.

STEVIE

Can you listen to me, please? The district manager came / in—

MARGARET

Okay, I understand. I've been late, and I won't be anymore. You can tell him I got the warning. *(Heads back inside)*

STEVIE

(Stops her) No, this isn't a warning. You've *had* warnings. I've given you seven warnings in the last two months.

MARGARET

You know I can't leave Joyce alone. You know that. She's like a baby. And Dottie doesn't always show up when she's supposed to. So what am I / supposed to—?

STEVIE

It's not like I have a choice in this. If I don't let you go then *I* get fired.

MARGARET

(Beat) What do you mean, let me go?

STEVIE

I told you it could happen.

MARGARET

Now, come / on—

STEVIE

Every week the district manager comes in to look at those punch cards.

MARGARET

I won't be late again. Tell him I promise.

STEVIE

I cover for you all the time, and he won't have it anymore. He wants me to let you go.

MARGARET

I'll get somebody else to look after Joyce.

STEVIE

That's what you always say.

MARGARET

(Beat) This is about the Chinese girl, isn't it.

STEVIE

No, and she's not Chinese.

MARGARET

She might be a little faster at the register, but she makes more mistakes.

STEVIE

First of all, she doesn't make mistakes. / Secondly—

MARGARET

She lives two blocks away! It's easier for her to get here on time!

STEVIE

Margaret, stop.

MARGARET

No, that guy comes in, and looks over your books, and who's getting paid what per hour—!

STEVIE

That's not what this is.

MARGARET

And because I've been here three years, I make a little bit more than the other girls, which costs the company a little bit more money—

STEVIE

You're not reliable.

MARGARET

You can't say that. I might be late once in a while but—

STEVIE

They don't want unreliable employees.

MARGARET

This is a *Dollar Store*. Who do they *think* is gonna work here?

STEVIE

Is that what I should tell them?

MARGARET

What they don't want is someone making nine-twenty an hour. And you know that's what this is.

STEVIE

I'll talk to my brother. Maybe he can get you something down at Gillette.

MARGARET

Gillette?

STEVIE

I'll call him this afternoon.

MARGARET

That's just your way of getting me out the door.

STEVIE

I'll call Jimmy, I swear to god.

MARGARET

He's not gonna call me in there. Besides, I've been to Gillette, it's all line work. I can't work a line, I'm too old for that. I can't keep up.

STEVIE

I'm trying to help you.

MARGARET

You wanna help me, let me go back to my register.

STEVIE

It's not my choice!

14

MARGARET

(Beat) I'll take a pay cut.

STEVIE

No. A pay cut? Margaret, listen to yourself.

MARGARET

I know the Chinese girl gets eight-sixty an hour, I can make do on that. It'll be tight, but I can do eight-sixty.

STEVIE

It's not about what you get paid.

MARGARET

That is bullshit. Pardon my French. But that is bullshit and you know it. I never asked for those raises. I only got them because you were required by law to give them to me. It wasn't much, god knows—a nickel here, fifteen cents one time—but I knew when I went over nine dollars, you were gonna start looking for an excuse to get rid of me.

STEVIE

You know that's not true.

MARGARET

Well if not you, then the district manager was. Or whoever adds up the numbers. Why pay *me* when you can give minimum wage to Chow Fun?

STEVIE

That doesn't help your case, you know. The racist stuff—

MARGARET

What racist stuff? That's her name.

STEVIE

(Writes something down) You know that's not her name.

MARGARET

You gonna put that in my file now? How I'm a racist?

STEVIE

You wouldn't even be out here if you weren't late.

MARGARET

And I wouldn't be late if I didn't have to beg someone to watch my daughter! And I wouldn't have to beg someone if I could *pay* someone, but you're making that very difficult, Stevie! *(Kicks the chair)*

STEVIE

Margaret—!

MARGARET

Please. Last time I got fired it took me seven months to find something, and that was when things weren't so bad. Now? Forget it. I won't be able to find *anything*.

STEVIE

Of course you will. You start asking around / and—

MARGARET

Eight-fifteen. You can lower me to eight-fifteen. That's what I started at. It's what you'd pay a new girl. Just pretend I'm a new girl. I can do eight-fifteen.

STEVIE

I can't. I can't do that. I'm sorry. It's just not working out.

MARGARET

(Beat) You're lucky your mother's dead.

16

STEVIE

(The discussion is over) All right.

MARGARET

We grew up together, me and your mother. If she knew what you were doing right now . . .

STEVIE

You know what, Margaret? I *do* actually remember that story about her stealing the turkey. But you know what you forgot? The part where you called the cops. You forgot how she spent Christmas Day down at Station Six. That was always how *I* heard it. You should ask my sisters how funny that story was.

MARGARET

(Beat) I didn't call the cops. Pat Moody called the cops.

STEVIE

(Moves to go back in) Okay.

MARGARET

I would never do that to your mother. Pat Moody called the cops. And they made her store manager. Because she was tough on shoplifters.

STEVIE

It doesn't matter.

MARGARET

Don't fire me, Stevie.

STEVIE

I have a job! What do you want me to do! I have to do my job!

MARGARET

(Beat) I know.

STEVIE

All right then. And stop with the: "You're lucky your mother's dead."

MARGARET

I was talking about you dating a Chinese girl. That's all. I don't think she'd approve.

(Stevie takes her in, then heads back inside, slamming the door behind him. Margaret is left alone.
Lights out.)

Scene 2

Margaret's kitchen, the next morning. It's small, and rundown. Her friend Jean, about fifty, and her landlady Dottie, mid-sixties, are here. Margaret, in the middle of a story, comes in from the next room with dirty dishes.

MARGARET

So he was on me as soon as I walked in. *(Puts dishes into the sink)*

DOTTIE

Who's this now?

JEAN

Stevie Grimes. At the Dollar Store.

DOTTIE

He works there?

JEAN

He's the young guy. He stands in the back of the store. He's up at bingo all the time.

DOTTIE

I can't picture him.

JEAN

He's the kid who stands in back of the store.

DOTTIE

The Dollar Store.

MARGARET

Yeah, the Dollar Store.

DOTTIE

Oh, I never go in there.

JEAN

Then you're not gonna know him, Dottie.

DOTTIE

That store's got nothing but shit in it.

MARGARET

Okay, well, that's who fired me.

(A TV suddenly blares from the next room.)

(Calls off) Turn it down, Joycey!

(The TV volume goes down again.)

JEAN

I always thought that was peculiar. Stevie at bingo.

MARGARET

He got it from his mother. Suzie was always up playing bingo.

DOTTIE

Suzie who?

MARGARET

Suzie Grimes. Stevie's mother.

DOTTIE

Suzie with the turkey?

MARGARET

Yeah.

DOTTIE

She was funny. "Who threw that bird at me?!" *(Laughs hard)* Remember that?

JEAN

Did you mention her? How you were friends?

MARGARET

It didn't matter to him.

DOTTIE

(Still amused) "Who threw that bird at me?!"

MARGARET

He kept blaming the district manager.

JEAN

That's how they do it. They blame the higher-ups.

(Again, the TV blares in the next room.)

MARGARET

(Calls off) Stop playing with those buttons. Joycey!

(The volume goes down again. Margaret makes them all instant coffee over the following.)

DOTTIE

It's not gonna be easy finding something, Margie. My Russell's been looking for work almost a year now.

JEAN

Yeah, well.

DOTTIE

What.

JEAN

Russell.

DOTTIE

What's that mean?

JEAN

Nothing. Just . . . Russell.

(The TV blares.)

MARGARET

Can you go in and turn that down for her, Dot?

(But Dottie doesn't move. The volume lowers anyway.)

DOTTIE

Russell's a good worker. He's just having trouble findin' something.

JEAN

Lucky that Franny works.

DOTTIE

That bitch. You know she won't even give him walking around money? All those years he spotted her cash when she was at hairdressin' school, and she won't hardly give him a nickel. But she's out buyin' cigarettes, and scratch tickets, and whatever else.

JEAN

It's her money.

DOTTIE

They're *married*. They're supposed to share.

JEAN

Then he should get a job.

DOTTIE

That's what I'm tellin' you, he *can't*. He's been trying.

JEAN

Russell can get a job. If Remy Hayes can get a job, Russell can.

DOTTIE

Who said anything about Remy Hayes?

JEAN

Well somebody hired *him*.

DOTTIE

So?

JEAN

So he's missin' half his face.

DOTTIE

And?

JEAN

And he's missin' half his face, Dottie! Whadaya mean, "And?"

MARGARET

He was such a good-lookin' kid too. Remember his mother passing around those pictures of him in his uniform?

JEAN

Then they sent him home with half a face.

MARGARET

Sad.

JEAN

And *still* he got a job at Jordan Marsh.

DOTTIE

Remy Hayes got a job because people feel bad for him. That's how he got a job. Russell didn't go to Iraq. Russell's not missing half his face. Nobody feels bad for Russell.

JEAN

You got that right.

(TV blares yet again.)

MARGARET

I'm gonna put her headphones on. *(Heads off to the next room)*

DOTTIE

(Regarding Margaret) And who's gonna hire *her*? I'm supposed to get rent at the end of the month. You think she's gonna give it to me?

24

JEAN

Well if you had showed up to watch Joyce.

DOTTIE

So it's my fault?

JEAN

She relies on you.

(The TV is silenced in the next room.)

DOTTIE

I don't *have* to watch her. I do it as a favor.

JEAN

What favor? She pays you fifty dollars a week.

DOTTIE

Like that's anything.

JEAN

You take it.

DOTTIE

Of course I take it. I'm watching her kid.

MARGARET

(Reentering) When you show up, you mean.

DOTTIE

Don't blame this on me, Margie. You know I have trouble getting up in the morning. I work nights after all.

JEAN

(Scoffs) You work nights.

25

DOTTIE

I *do* work nights.

JEAN

You're upstairs.

DOTTIE

Yeah, *working*. I make my crafts.

JEAN

Gimme a break, those stupid rabbit things—

DOTTIE

That's my *work*.

JEAN

You glue Styrofoam balls onto flowerpots.

DOTTIE

I get five bucks a pop for those rabbits. People like 'em.

JEAN

Then they're morons.

MARGARET

I think those rabbits are cute.

JEAN

Five bucks for forty cents of crap.

DOTTIE

It's not crap.

JEAN

I hate to break it to ya, Dottie, but anything with googly eyes is crap.

DOTTIE

Oh fuck off.

MARGARET

She sells a lot of those rabbits up at bingo.

DOTTIE

And with Easter coming up, this is kinda my high season.

JEAN

(Laughs) High season.

DOTTIE

It *is*! So watching Joyce all day, then working on my crafts all night, *yes* sometimes I have trouble getting up in the morning, but Margie knew that.

MARGARET

It's not your fault, Dottie.

JEAN

Of course it is! Don't let her off the hook like that!

MARGARET

Let it go.

JEAN

No, you're too nice. That's why you don't have anything.

MARGARET

Oh, is that why?

JEAN

Yeah, you have to be a selfish prick to get anywhere.

MARGARET

I hate when people say that. You know it's not true, Jean.

JEAN

No? Look at Dottie.

DOTTIE

What do you mean look at Dottie?

JEAN

You think she cares about you? No. I bet if you threatened to not pay her that babysitting money, she would've showed up on time. That's what she would've done to *you*. Maybe you should start acting like her.

MARGARET

That's not who I am.

JEAN

No I know, you invite her in for coffee instead: "Hey, thanks for gettin' me fired."

DOTTIE

I did not get her fired!

MARGARET

She's right, Jeannie. Now stop stirring / the shit.

DOTTIE

If you wanna get someone else to watch Joyce—

MARGARET

I don't.

JEAN

Why not? I'll do it. All you do is sit and watch TV. How hard is that? To sit in there with her and watch soaps.

DOTTIE

That's not all it is.

JEAN

No, I know, you put her to work sometimes, too.

DOTTIE

What are you talkin' about?

JEAN

Making those rabbits. Margie told me.

MARGARET

Joyce likes doing that.

DOTTIE

I let her put on the heads, that's all. It's fun for her.

JEAN

Oh, okay.

DOTTIE

And I have to redo most of 'em because she puts them on *lopsided*! So don't / act like—

JEAN

You got your own little *sweatshop* down here.

DOTTIE

Why don't you go home?

JEAN

Because Margie made me coffee. I wanna enjoy it.

DOTTIE

Then stop causin' trouble. Talkin' about sweatshops and tryin' to tell me how easy it is to watch Joyce. Have you ever tried to give her lunch, Jean? She's worse than a baby! The mess—

MARGARET

She's right.

DOTTIE

And if she gets mad, or upset about whatever, she has a fit. I can't just leave her here, she'd hurt herself.

MARGARET

I appreciate you looking out for her.

DOTTIE

It's not fun. I could be upstairs in my *own* apartment watching TV, I don't need to be down here. I got punched last week.

MARGARET

By accident.

DOTTIE

Accident or no, it didn't tickle. She's as big as a grown man, and when she starts throwing those arms / around—

JEAN

All right, Dottie.

DOTTIE

Well you started it, trying to tell me how easy my job is. Saying Margie got fired because of me. You think I wanted her to lose her job? How am I gonna get my rent if she don't have a paycheck coming in?

JEAN

You'll get your rent. She'll find a job / and you'll—

DOTTIE

Where? You think everybody can get a job! Not everybody is Remy fuckin' Hayes!

MARGARET

All right.

DOTTIE

Not everybody had half their face blown off!

JEAN

Well then maybe she should start making rabbits!

DOTTIE

(Pointed) She better *not.* *(After a beat)* You can go down Gillette, Margie. Have you tried down there?

MARGARET

Gillette's not gonna hire me. Lorraine Feeney went down there last month, and they hardly looked at her application. And she's ten years younger than I am.

DOTTIE

Lorraine Feeney's got a record. They don't like to hire people who've been in prison.

JEAN

What are you talking about? Half the Politos work down there. Do you know how many of *them* did time?

31

MARGARET

I'm not going to Gillette. *(To Jean)* You think Chucky might have something for me?

JEAN

He just cut me down to two shifts a week. I'm looking to pick up something myself. You don't wanna work banquets anyway. Not with your back. Those platters? Forget it.

MARGARET

I'm gonna be the next Cookie McDermott.

JEAN

God forbid.

MARGARET

(Laughs) I am. The way I'm headed.

DOTTIE

Who's that?

JEAN

Cookie. The one up by the bank. She's got the granny cart.

MARGARET

We went to school with her.

DOTTIE

The wino in the sun hat?

MARGARET

That's what happened after her husband died. Left her with nothing. Now she sleeps against that wall.

DOTTIE

That's no life.

MARGARET

(Laughing) Maybe me and Joyce can move in next to her.

JEAN

Stop it.

MARGARET

"Scoot on over, wouldja, Cookie?"

JEAN

Poor thing.

MARGARET

Don't say poor thing. Me and Cookie are gonna have a grand ol' time, passing that bottle back and forth.

DOTTIE

They should get her outta there. That Cookie lady. It's not right. Her sleeping on the sidewalk. It makes the neighborhood look bad.

JEAN

(Beat. Trying to sound offhand) You know who you should ask for a job?

MARGARET

Who.

JEAN

Mikey Dillon.

MARGARET

(Beat) What?

JEAN

Yeah, why not?

MARGARET

Why would you mention him of all people?

JEAN

You just reminded me. All that Cookie talk. They were buddies, right?

MARGARET

Not really.

JEAN

He hung out with her brother though.

MARGARET

So?

JEAN

So I ran into him. Didn't I tell you?

MARGARET

(Beat) No.

JEAN

Yeah, Mikey Dillon. I shoulda told you— *That's* who you should hit up.

DOTTIE

Who's this now?

MARGARET

Just a kid we grew up with.

DOTTIE

Kevin Dillon?

JEAN

No—*Mikey* Dillon He lived down Old Harbor.

DOTTIE

His wife works up the clinic?

JEAN

That's Kevin Dillon. It's no relation.

MARGARET

Where'dya see him?

JEAN

At the hotel. One of the luncheons we did.

MARGARET

Oh yeah? He was a guest?

JEAN

It was for the Boys and Girls Clubs. Every year they give these medals to the kids for being good, or not killing each other, or whatever. And he was one of the speakers.

MARGARET

No shit.

JEAN

Yeah, him and one of the Bruins. Because they were in the Clubs when they were kids, so they're like the success stories. And they tell the kids to work hard and stay in school, or whatever. Be all you can be.

MARGARET

Mikey Dillon.

JEAN

Yeah. I saw the name tag, and did a double take. I wasn't sure it
was him, it's been so long.

MARGARET

He got old?

JEAN

Not really. He looks good. He was shocked to see me though. I was
like, "Ya remember me, Doctor?" Ya know he's a doctor, right?

MARGARET

I heard that.

JEAN

Yeah, that's why he was there. As an example for the kids. They
only cared about the hockey player though. He's downtown, he
said. He does something with babies.

MARGARET

A baby doctor?

JEAN

No, something else. I wasn't really listening to tell ya the truth.
I didn't want to get in trouble for talking to the guests, so . . .

MARGARET

Wow, Mikey Dillon. *(Processes that)* Did he ask about me?

JEAN

It was just a quick talk. He looks good though. You should go
down there. Tell him you need a job.

MARGARET

(Laughs) Right.

JEAN

I'm serious.

MARGARET

How am I gonna get a job in a doctor's office?

JEAN

I don't know, answering phones or something. Ask him what he's got available. Southie pride, right? Maybe he'll cut ya a break.

DOTTIE

Was this the kid who stole the bread truck?

JEAN

No, that's *Kevin* Dillon. Would you shut up? We're talking about a totally different person. You *don't know him*.

MARGARET

He was always good people. Mikey.

JEAN

Uh-huh.

MARGARET

He *was*.

JEAN

Okay.

MARGARET

I thought he was living in Pennsylvania or someplace.

JEAN

D.C., he said. He's been back a while though.

MARGARET

Dr. Dillon.

JEAN

I know, right? Southie doctor. That must be a first.

DOTTIE

Peggy Ford's daughter is a doctor.

JEAN

No she's not. She's a vet's assistant. She holds the dogs down when they're put to sleep.

DOTTIE

Oh.

JEAN

Now there's a job Russell should look into.

DOTTIE

Killing dogs?

JEAN

He'd be perfect for that.

DOTTIE

You're an asshole.

MARGARET

Mikey Dillon, huh?

JEAN

You should call him.

MARGARET

I haven't seen him in a hundred years.

JEAN

You should call him anyway, just to see what he says.

MARGARET

He's not gonna hire me.

DOTTIE

(Heads for the door) Someone better. You can't stay here for nothin', Margie. You know I like you and Joycey both, but—

MARGARET

Can you stop, please? I said I'd pay you, so shut up about it.

DOTTIE

(Beat) I'm upstairs if you need me. *(Exits)*

JEAN

You should call him, Margie. Ya never know.

(Lights out.)

Scene 3

Lights up on Dr. Michael Dillon's office. Tastefully decorated. A couple of family photos on a shelf behind his desk. Mike, about fifty, handsome, is working at his desk. After a couple beats Margaret peeks in.

MARGARET

Mike?

MIKE

(Comes to the door) There you are!

MARGARET

How you doin'?

MIKE

Come on in!

(She comes in. He gives her a hug.)

40

Holy Jesus. Margie Walsh.

MARGARET

Hi, Mike.

MIKE

From Prehistoric Times.

MARGARET

Just about.

(He's a little too amiable. She's a bit uncomfortable.)

MIKE

Sorry you had to wait out there, I was on the line with the caterer.

MARGARET

It's okay.

MIKE

My wife's throwing this party, so there are all these questions about / the menu.

MARGARET

I hope it's okay that I came in without an appointment or / anything.

MIKE

It's fine. I had some cancellations, which never happens / so—

MARGARET

Yeah, they said.

MIKE

You got lucky.

MARGARET

Is the party for you?

MIKE

The party?

MARGARET

You said your wife was / throwing a party.

MIKE

Oh, yeah, it's my birthday this weekend—

MARGARET

March 22nd.

MIKE

(Beat) That's right. Anyway, she lives for that stuff. Any excuse to throw a party.

MARGARET

That's nice.

MIKE

I'm really sorry you had to wait.

MARGARET

I wouldn't have come down, but I called a few times on Monday, and then again yesterday, but they wouldn't put me through.

MIKE

They do that if I'm with patients.

MARGARET

I didn't want to be a pest about it.

MIKE

It's totally fine. How you doin'?

MARGARET

I'm okay.

MIKE

Still in Southie?

MARGARET

Yeah, down on Tudor Street.

MIKE

The Lower End.

MARGARET

Lower End.

MIKE

Same as always.

MARGARET

I guess.

MIKE

This is crazy. Look at you.

MARGARET

I'm fat.

MIKE

You are not.

MARGARET

Well, I'm not seventeen.

43

MIKE

No, nobody's seventeen. How's Gobie?

MARGARET

Oh, he's, uh, down in Virginia somewhere.

MIKE

Oh yeah?

MARGARET

Or Georgia, I guess. Somewhere down there. Last I heard.

MIKE

Well say hi to him from me.

MARGARET

Okay. We haven't heard from him in / a while.

MIKE

Did you ever marry him?

MARGARET

Oh god, no.

MIKE

You were together a while though.

MARGARET

Not really.

MIKE

Well tell him I say hello. *(Laughing)* I think he owes me a few bucks.

MARGARET

We don't really— He could be / dead for all I know.

MIKE

(Laughing) That deadbeat was always— What'd you say?

MARGARET

I said he could be dead for all I know.

MIKE

Oh.

MARGARET

We've lost touch.

MIKE

That's too bad.

MARGARET

Not really.

MIKE

Oh, okay.

(Silence.)

MARGARET

So Jeannie said she ran into you. At the luncheon thing.

MIKE

Yeah, she's the same, huh?

MARGARET

Yeah.

MIKE

Mouthy from Southie.

45

MARGARET

(Little chuckle) Yeah.

MIKE

I would've known her anywhere.

MARGARET

I heard you were a doctor, but I didn't know if it was true or not.

MIKE

It's true.

MARGARET

That is awesome.

MIKE

Oh, thanks.

MARGARET

I never would've guessed that.

MIKE

No?

MARGARET

I mean, I knew you were smart. Everybody knew that, but I would never have pictured you delivering babies.

MIKE

I don't actually deliver the babies.

MARGARET

You don't?

MIKE

I mean, I *have* in the past but— I'm a reproductive endocrinologist.

MARGARET

I don't know what you just said, but I just got a little excited.

MIKE

(Chuckles) Okay.

MARGARET

Was that even English?

MIKE

I do fertility stuff.

MARGARET

You should've just said that.

MIKE

And I help with high-risk pregnancies.

MARGARET

I only went to Southie High after all. You can't be using those five-dollar words on me.

MIKE

Sorry.

MARGARET

I'm just playin' with you.

MIKE

You asked what I did.

MARGARET

I know, I was kidding.

MIKE

Okay. I mean, I went to Southie High, too.

47

MARGARET

Yeah, and U-Penn, and wherever else.

MIKE

Right.

MARGARET

I didn't go to U-Penn.

MIKE

No, I know.

MARGARET

(Chuckles) I didn't go to U-Anywhere. *(Pause)* A doctor, though. I think that's awesome.

MIKE

Thank you.

MARGARET

You're the only doctor I know. In real life, I mean.

MIKE

Real life?

MARGARET

Not somebody I *go* to, in other words. You know what I mean.

MIKE

Yeah. Personally.

MARGARET

Personally. Exactly.

(Silence.)

MIKE

So, are you pregnant, / or—

MARGARET

No. God. Am I / *pregnant?*

MIKE

I'm just pulling your leg.

MARGARET

Oh. I thought you were really / asking me.

MIKE

Although, we've had some older moms in here. You'd be surprised.
Almost fifty, some of them.

MARGARET

I'm not pregnant.

MIKE

No, I know.

MARGARET

(Beat) So you got the messages then?

MIKE

Yeah, the receptionist played them for me.

MARGARET

Then you know why / I—

MIKE

Yes, I was just—

MARGARET

I didn't mean to bug you about it.

MIKE

No, I should've called you back. This is the first slow day we've had.

MARGARET

It's just, my landlady's tapping her foot for the rent, / so—

MIKE

No, I know.

MARGARET

I wouldn't have come, but I didn't know if you were getting the messages.

MIKE

No, I got them.

MARGARET

So Jeannie said I should just come down here.

MIKE

The trouble is, Margie, I don't have anything open right now.

MARGARET

(Beat) No, I figured.

MIKE

And you saw, we don't have a lot of people out there.

MARGARET

No, I know.

MIKE

Just a couple girls answering the phones.

MARGARET

Right.

MIKE

Have you even worked one of those systems? You have to know /
how to—

MARGARET

It wouldn't *have* to be answering the phones. I just mentioned the
phones because I didn't know what you might have.

MIKE

I see.

MARGARET

I could do whatever. Janitorial stuff or—

MIKE

We have a service that does that. A cleaning service. They come
at night.

MARGARET

Oh, I couldn't do nights I don't think. Not with my Joyce.

MIKE

(Beat) I have nothing to do with the cleaning folks anyway. They
hire their own people.

MARGARET

That's okay, I couldn't do nights. I just didn't know what the jobs
are in a doctor's office. I don't know if there's filing or whatever?

MIKE

That's what I'm saying, I don't have anything.

MARGARET

Right.

MIKE

I'm sorry. I should've called you back.

MARGARET

I knew it was a long shot. I only came down because Jean said she ran into you. I told her it was stupid.

MIKE

Have you tried Gillette?

MARGARET

(A wry chuckle) Yeah.

MIKE

Back in the day everybody worked down Gillette. Is that place still open?

MARGARET

Oh, yeah, they're open.

MIKE

I'm sorry, Margie.

MARGARET

That's okay.

MIKE

If I hear about anything, I'll definitely call you. I have your number now.

(This is probably the time she should leave. But she doesn't.)

MARGARET

(Regarding a photo over his shoulder) Is that your family?

MIKE

Yeah.

MARGARET

Can I see?

MIKE

(Slightest pause) Sure.

MARGARET

You don't want to show me?

MIKE

(Hands her the photo) Of course. I don't care / if—

MARGARET

(A little laugh) I'm not gonna *stalk* them.

MIKE

It's just an old photo, that's all. That's in D.C. We were there for a while, so . . .

MARGARET

(Pause as she takes in the photo) Your wife is beautiful.

MIKE

Thank you.

MARGARET

And young.

MIKE

Oh. Not really. Like, I said it's an old picture.

MARGARET

How old?

MIKE

I don't know. Three years.

MARGARET

So, it's not *that* old. She's still young.

MIKE

Younger than me, yeah. A little bit.

MARGARET

(A little chuckle) "A little bit." Okay.

MIKE

I waited a while. To settle down.

MARGARET

Well she's beautiful. Your daughter, too.

MIKE

Thank you. She's six now.

MARGARET

Your wife?

MIKE

You're funny.

MARGARET

(Hands the photo back) She *is* beautiful though. They both are. Everybody's beautiful.

MIKE

Thank you. *(Beat)* How's *your* little girl?

MARGARET

Little girl. Now who's funny? My little girl's older than your wife.

MIKE

Not quite.

MARGARET

Well she's not a little girl.

MIKE

No, I know. *(Beat)* You know, my sister-in-law had a premature baby. Not as premature as . . .

MARGARET

Joyce.

MIKE

Joyce, right, but she had some troubles, too. She's doing better though.

MARGARET

That's good. Mine's not.

MIKE

Sorry. And Gobie doesn't help out?

MARGARET

No.

MIKE

That surprises me. He always seemed like a stand-up guy.

MARGARET

Well he's not. Honestly, though? It's better he's not around. Or it *would* be, if I had a job.

MIKE

I'm sorry, Margie. I wish I had something. *(Puts on his doctor's coat)*

MARGARET

I know. Nobody does. I went up and down Broadway, and put applications in *everywhere*. Nobody's calling me though. I even went online. Up at the library. You can apply for jobs online now.

MIKE

Oh yeah?

MARGARET

I *think* I did it right, but I don't know. I'm always so stupid when it comes to computers. And those librarians won't help. They're *supposed* to but— Anyway, I think I did it right. Nobody's calling though.

MIKE

You gotta give it time. Just keep putting yourself out / there.

MARGARET

You know it doesn't have to be full-time, right? I could fill in, like if somebody gets sick or whatever. Or if you need somebody to work weekends?

MIKE

That's not how we do it, Margie.

MARGARET

Okay. I figured. That's fine.

MIKE

I swear, I'm not holding out on you.

MARGARET

No, I know. *(Beat)* I wouldn't fit in here anyway.

MIKE

What do you mean?

MARGARET

In the office. It's . . . you know.

MIKE

Formal?

MARGARET

Formal, yeah. That's a good word for it.

MIKE

It's just a doctor's office.

MARGARET

No, I know. I don't think I'd be comfortable, is all. And that Spanish girl at the desk was pretty cunty to me.

MIKE

(Chuckles) Yikes.

MARGARET

Pardon my French. But she was giving me some attitude.

MIKE

Denise was?

MARGARET

You obviously hired her for her looks, and not her friendly demeanor.

MIKE

I didn't hire her because of her looks.

MARGARET

No? Because she's very pretty. And she's got a whole lot of boobs goin' on.

MIKE

She's also very good at her job.

MARGARET

I guess. If her job means being rude to people. She was all suspicious, asking me these questions.

MIKE

Well, when you walk in off the street / like that—

MARGARET

I told her we were friends though.

MIKE

I know.

MARGARET

What I wanted to say is, "Mind your business, bitch."

MIKE

It's probably good you didn't.

MARGARET

She really didn't want me coming back here.

MIKE

Well, you got back here anyway. It was / good to see you.

MARGARET

Anyway, that's what I meant. She and I wouldn't have gotten along, I don't think, so it's probably for the best you don't have a job for me. I'm not fancy enough for this office. You're all lace-curtain Irish now.

MIKE

(Beat) What?

MARGARET

You *are*, it's great. I'm happy for you.

MIKE

What do you mean, "lace-curtain."

MARGARET

What do *you* call it? "My wife is throwing me a party."

MIKE

What, you don't throw parties?

MARGARET

Not really. Not *catered*.

MIKE

It's a special— It's not like we do it all the time.

MARGARET

You don't have to get defensive. I was just saying. You're not . . .

MIKE

What.

MARGARET

Southie at all.

MIKE

Ouch.

MARGARET

You wouldn't know that that's where you're from, I'm saying.

MIKE

So I've lost my street cred.

MARGARET

No, I think it's awesome.

MIKE

Yeah, you keep saying that, but I'm starting to not believe you.

MARGARET

I *do* think it's awesome. You're like someone on a TV show.

MIKE

Uh-huh.

MARGARET

You *are*. You know what I mean. Professional.

MIKE

All right, professional I don't mind, but lace-curtain . . .

MARGARET

It just means you did good.

MIKE

No it doesn't. I haven't been in the neighborhood for a while, but I remember what lace-curtain means.

MARGARET

It's a good thing, Mike.

MIKE

No it isn't. It means I think I'm better than other people.

MARGARET

That's not what it means.

MIKE

Yes it does.

MARGARET

Well, that's not how *I* mean it.

MIKE

The old-timers called the Kennedys' lace-curtain: "Aw, they don't care about us. They're all lace-curtain now."

MARGARET

Well, I don't know anything about that.

MIKE

Or when a union boss or whoever moved out to Wellesley.

MARGARET

Where do *you* live?

MIKE

(Beat) Not Wellesley.

MARGARET

Brookline?

(No response.)

Weston?

MIKE

(Beat) Chestnut Hill.

MARGARET

(Laughs) You're not lace-curtain though. Kid grows up in the Old Harbor Projects—

MIKE

Okay.

61

MARGARET

—moves to Chestnut Hill.

MIKE

Okay.

MARGARET

Chestnut Hill!

MIKE

I'm still a Southie kid at heart though.

MARGARET

Are ya?

MIKE

Yes.

MARGARET

Chestnut Hill. That's nice. Not that I've ever been there. But it *sounds* nice. *Chestnut Hill.* Big house?

MIKE

It's all right.

MARGARET

Humble. I bet it's awesome. That's all I ever wanted—a big house somewhere. You got trees?

MIKE

A couple.

MARGARET

Sounds nice. Ya got a guest room?

(They sort of laugh.)

Mikey Dillon. You're rich!

MIKE

Take it easy.

MARGARET

You *are*! You're *rich*!

MIKE

I'm not rich.

MARGARET

Well what would *you* call it?

MIKE

I don't know.

MARGARET

Wealthy?

MIKE

We're just . . . comfortable.

MARGARET

Oh, comfortable.

MIKE

Yeah.

MARGARET

You're comfortable. Okay. I guess that makes me *un*-comfortable
then. Is that what you call us lowly folk? *Un*-comfortable?

MIKE

Nope.

MARGARET

You're comfortable. I like that. It's nicer than rich. And you *look* comfortable.

MIKE

Funny, I don't feel comfortable at this particular moment.

MARGARET

I'm sorry. It's not polite to talk money, is it. Us Southie kids forget that sometimes.

MIKE

Right.

MARGARET

(Beat) You ever get back there at all? Walk the Sugar Bowl? Grab a clam roll at Sully's?

MIKE

Not really.

MARGARET

How come?

MIKE

(Beat) My parents moved to Florida, so there was never a reason to . . .

MARGARET

Go back?

MIKE

I don't know. I should though. I miss those clam rolls.

MARGARET

Huh. Well they're still there.

MIKE

I've been doing some work with the Boys and Girls Clubs though. I'm on the board, so . . .

MARGARET

(A little laugh) You're on the board.

MIKE

And I still have cousins in Southie.

MARGARET

The Feeneys?

MIKE

Yeah.

MARGARET

(Knowing) Close to them, are ya?

MIKE

Well . . .

MARGARET

They gonna be at your party?

MIKE

(Chuckles) You know I was never tight with the Feeneys. But that's my father's fault.

MARGARET

You still have ties though. You're still Mikey Dee from Old Harbor.

MIKE

If I was close to the Feeneys they would come to the party.

MARGARET

Oh, yeah? You'd let the Southie rats in?

MIKE

What are you doing? Do you think I'm lying about the job?

MARGARET

No.

MIKE

Then why are you being so passive-aggressive?

MARGARET

Okay, Big Words.

MIKE

I think you're deliberately needling me.

MARGARET

What I say?

MIKE

Did you get mean, Margie?

MARGARET

(Beat) No.

MIKE

Southie girls could be so mean. I remember how hard they were. Your friend Jeannie? Forget it. She could beat the shit out of me.

MARGARET

Still could.

MIKE

You were never like that though. I hope you're still nice, Margie.

MARGARET

You think I'm not? Because I called you lace-curtain?

MIKE

I can't tell.

MARGARET

Because I asked if you invited the Feeneys?

MIKE

If the Feeneys wanna come, they can come.

MARGARET

I'll let 'em know. *(Beat)* Can I come, too?

MIKE

(A nervous laugh) Ha.

MARGARET

Is that a yes?

MIKE

You don't wanna come to *this* party, believe me. You'd be bored out of your mind. Bunch of stuffy doctors and their stuffy wives.

MARGARET

Sounds like you need me to liven things up.

MIKE

You'd certainly do that.

MARGARET

Any of these people hiring, ya think?

MIKE

Aw, and here I thought you wanted to celebrate my birthday.

MARGARET

Well that, too.

MIKE

I'm just a *Job Fair* to you.

MARGARET

You know I'm not fussy, Mikey. I'll clean their pools if that's what they got. No shame in an honest job.

MIKE

I don't think I know anybody with a pool.

MARGARET

You just don't want me minglin' with your buddies. You afraid I might embarrass you?

MIKE

Is that who you think I am?

MARGARET

I don't know.

MIKE

You're actually starting to offend me a little bit with all this lace-curtain stuff.

MARGARET

Come on, I'm just playing.

MIKE

You wouldn't embarrass me.

MARGARET

No, I know. You're a good guy, Mikey. I'm just bustin' balls. You're good people. I always said that about you. *(Beat)* You *are* good people, right?

MIKE

I like to think so.

MARGARET

Of course you are. Helping these babies in here. The nervous parents. Volunteering at the Boys Club, or whatever it is you do. Donate money?

MIKE

(Beat) A little bit.

MARGARET

See, that's a good guy. Giving money to these kids who you don't even *know*. That's good people. I know you'd help me if you could. I know you would.

MIKE

(Beat) You know you're welcome to come, Margie. If the party's *that* interesting / to you—

MARGARET

Oh, now I get to come.

MIKE

I never said you couldn't come.

MARGARET

What I do, bruise your pride?

MIKE

Yeah, actually, but I'm gonna overlook that and invite you anyway.

MARGARET

No, not if I have to guilt you into it.

MIKE

You're not. I'll tell Denise to give you directions right now.

MARGARET

The Spanish girl with the boobies?

MIKE

She's Dominican, but yeah.

MARGARET

Nah, that's okay. I'll let ya off the hook.

MIKE

(Beat. Realizes) I see what this is.

MARGARET

What.

MIKE

You don't actually want to come. You just want me to feel bad.

MARGARET

Why would I want that?

MIKE

I don't know. But it's weird how you suddenly don't want to come to the party after all. I know Chestnut Hill's a scary place—

MARGARET

You got that right. All that money in one town?

MIKE

Suddenly you don't want to hang out with my boring friends.

MARGARET

I'll hang out, I don't care. So long as they wanna gimme a job.
They gonna gimme a job?

MIKE

Somebody might. A couple of those guys have done stupider
things. But you don't wanna come now.

MARGARET

You think I won't?

MIKE

No, I think you'll say you will, then call the next day, and leave a
message saying your kid got sick or something.

MARGARET

Hey, I just wanted a job, Mikey. But if you wanna play a game a
chicken that's fine, too.

MIKE

I'm not playing anything.

MARGARET

Stop fucking with me.

MIKE

I'm not.

MARGARET

'Cause you're very close to hurting my feelings.

MIKE

Hurting *your* feelings? Seriously, Margie, if you want to come you
should come, but stop trying to make me out to be this jackass
who's forgotten where he's come from.

71

MARGARET

(Beat) When is it?

MIKE

Saturday night.

MARGARET

I happen to be free Saturday night.

MIKE

I'm not surprised.

MARGARET

Now why don't you buzz your girl and tell her I'd like directions.

MIKE

(Slightest pause) You're not gonna come.

MARGARET

I am *now*.

MIKE

Okay.

(He reaches for the phone and dials Denise's extension.)

MARGARET

You don't want me to.

MIKE

I just invited you, didn't I? *(Into phone)* Hey Denise, could you print out directions to my house for Miss Walsh? She'll be coming to the party on Saturday. *(Denise says something funny, he chuckles)* No, you cannot.

MARGARET

I'll be taking the T.

MIKE

(Into the phone) T directions . . . yeah. Thank you. *(Hangs up)*
 Hope you like salmon.

MARGARET

Never had it.

MIKE

Well, you're gonna.

MARGARET

(Moves to go) All right. This was fun, Mike. Thanks for letting me in.

MIKE

Like I had a choice.

MARGARET

(Laughs) Yeah.

(She heads for the door, then turns back.)

If you hear of anything in the meantime, call me though, okay?
About work? I'll do whatever.

MIKE

Okay.

MARGARET

See you Saturday.

MIKE

Will I?

MARGARET

Oh yeah. You're in deep now, Doctor.

*(Margaret goes. Mike is left alone.
 Lights out.)*

Scene 4

Margaret, Jean and Dottie are at a folding table in the basement of a church. They're playing bingo. We hear the murmur of the crowd, and the voice of a priest calling the bingo numbers over a cheap sound system.

The women, bingo daubers in hand, play their cards. The cards are on rip-off sheets. Margaret has one sheet of three cards. The others are playing twelve or fifteen cards at a time. They'll be playing and daubing their cards through much of this scene. Dottie has several of her crafted rabbits on display in front of her. They are for sale.

VOICE OF PRIEST

I-17. I . . . 17.

(They play.)

B-11.

                    DOTTIE

They gave me shit cards.

                VOICE OF PRIEST

B . . . 11.

                    DOTTIE

(Leans over to Jean) You got anything?

                     JEAN

Are you kidding?

                    DOTTIE

They always give me shit cards.

                   MARGARET

I'm down to two numbers.

                    DOTTIE

You're down to two?

                     JEAN

Oooh, Margie's got a little heat under her.

                    DOTTIE

I find it awful strange that someone with no money can afford bingo.

                   MARGARET

Jean treated me. If I win, we're splitting it.

                    DOTTIE

Huh.

                     JEAN

It's just a few cards.

                      75

VOICE OF PRIEST

O-70. O . . . 70.

JEAN

He looked good, right?

DOTTIE

Who did?

JEAN

Mikey Dillon. *(To Margaret)* You did good, Margie, going down there.

MARGARET

Tell me that after the party.

JEAN

It's gonna go great.

DOTTIE

Or it won't.

VOICE OF PRIEST

B-3. B . . . 3.

DOTTIE

Who's with Joyce?

MARGARET

Ruthie.

DOTTIE

Ruthie? How ya payin' her?

JEAN

You think she's hiding money from you, Dottie?

MARGARET

I'm not paying Ruthie anything. Her TV fried, so her kids are goin' nuts. I said she could come over and use mine if she watched Joyce.

JEAN

Ruthie's kids are animals.

MARGARET

Joyce likes 'em.

DOTTIE

Joyce likes everybody, god love her.

VOICE OF PRIEST

G-48. G . . . 48.

MARGARET

You think we jinxed her?

JEAN

Who.

MARGARET

Cookie McDermott.

JEAN

Oh my god, would you quit with that?

MARGARET

You don't think it's spooky though? That we were making fun of her?

JEAN

We weren't making fun of her.

MARGARET

Then a few days later she dies up there?

JEAN

I'm surprised she lasted as long as she did actually. Lying on the ground months at a time, exposed to the elements like that. Cookie was a fuckin' wreck.

VOICE OF PRIEST

N-31.

JEAN

Way before she lived on that wall even.

VOICE OF PRIEST

N . . . 31.

MARGARET

You don't think it's spooky though?

DOTTIE

I do. I think it's spooky. I think you people are witches.

MARGARET

Sissy said she was layin' there for two days before anyone did anything. They thought she was sleepin'.

VOICE OF PRIEST

O-74.

MARGARET

Two days, and nobody noticed. That's pretty sad.

VOICE OF PRIEST

O . . . 74.

DOTTIE

These cards are terrible. I think they see me comin' and say, "Oh here comes Dottie, give *her* the shit cards."

MARGARET

I'm waiting now.

JEAN

You are?

MARGARET

G-53.

JEAN

Come on, G-53.

MARGARET

If I hit tonight, I'm gonna buy a nice party outfit.

DOTTIE

What do you need a new outfit for? Those people aren't gonna hire you.

JEAN

Why are you so negative all the time?

VOICE OF PRIEST

G-59.

DOTTIE

I'm not negative, I'm realistic.

VOICE OF PRIEST

G . . . 59.

MARGARET

He said somebody might be hiring.

DOTTIE

Who?

MARGARET

He didn't say who.

DOTTIE

Which means nobody. You're gonna go all the way out / there—

JEAN

What do you care where she goes?

DOTTIE

I don't, I'm just saying it sounds unlikely.

MARGARET

I wanna see his house anyway. I'm curious. I bet it's nice. And if somebody wants to give me a job while I'm there, so be it.

DOTTIE

And what if they don't?

VOICE OF PRIEST

I-20.

JEAN

I know what *I'd* do.

MARGARET

What.

VOICE OF PRIEST

I . . . 20.

JEAN

I'd say Joyce wasn't premature.

MARGARET

(Beat) What are you talking about?

JEAN

Joyce. If she wasn't premature then the math almost works out.

MARGARET

Jesus, Jeannie.

JEAN

That's what I'd do. Pull a Maury Povich on his ass.

DOTTIE

What does *that* mean?

JEAN

It means she whips out a picture of Joyce and tells him he has a long-lost daughter.

VOICE OF PRIEST

O-63.

JEAN

You say, "Hey, Mike, you remember that summer we dated?"

VOICE OF PRIEST

O . . . 63.

DOTTIE

You dated?

MARGARET

No, we / didn't—

81

JEAN

Yes you *did*, right before Gobie.

MARGARET

Just a few *weeks*, Jean. Don't be stupid.

JEAN

That's all it takes! If Joyce wasn't premature—

MARGARET

But she *was*.

JEAN

I'd walk her right up to the front door.

VOICE OF PRIEST

I-16.

MARGARET

(Laughs) You *would*, too.

VOICE OF PRIEST

I . . . 16.

JEAN

Damn straight, I would. You gotta start thinking like other people do. Get him to pay some of that child support Gobie refuses to cough up.

MARGARET

(Laughs) You are too much.

VOICE OF PRIEST

G-51.

JEAN

Jesus. He's calling all around you, Margie.

VOICE OF PRIEST

G . . . 51.

JEAN

53, Father! / We're looking for 53!

MARGARET

Don't do that, you're gonna get these old biddies mad.

JEAN

We gotta buy this girl an outfit!

MARGARET

Shut up.

DOTTIE

You know Helen Feeney did something like that.

JEAN

Like what?

DOTTIE

That Maury Povich thing. She made Bob Swanson believe those boys were actually his.

VOICE OF PRIEST

B-13.

DOTTIE

Why he'd ever believe her is beyond me.

VOICE OF PRIEST

B . . . 13.

DOTTIE

You take one look at those boys, and you *know* they're Mexican. And I said that to him, too. Up at the VFW one night.

MARGARET

No, you didn't.

DOTTIE

Yes I did. I said, "Bob, those boys are Mexican." And he said, "Shut up, Dottie. They don't look like no Mexicans," and I said "Well you've never seen a Mexican then. Because those kids are straight off the taco truck." And then he got crazy mad, and I was asked to leave.

VOICE OF PRIEST

N-41.

JEAN

(To Margaret) Well there ya go.

VOICE OF PRIEST

N . . . 41.

JEAN

Worked on Bob Swanson, it could work on Mikey Dillon.

MARGARET

Let's just stick with the job.

DOTTIE

What job? Nobody goes to a fancy party lookin' to hire an unemployed cashier.

MARGARET

Ya never know, Dottie. People have wanted crazier things.

JEAN

Yeah, those stupid rabbits for example.

VOICE OF PRIEST

G-55.

VOICE OF OLD LADY

Bingo!

(A collective groan from the crowd.)

DOTTIE	MARGARET	JEAN
Sonofabitch.	Damnit all.	Mother*fuck*er.

VOICE OF PRIEST

Check that card, Helen.

JEAN

Win the next one, wouldja Margie? So you can give this nut her
damn money.

VOICE OF PRIEST

That's a good bingo.

*(The women tear off their top sheets of bingo cards and crumple them
up, revealing the next game. Stevie from the Dollar Store wanders over
with a fistful of bingo sheets, looking for a seat.)*

JEAN

Well, look who it is.

(Stevie sees Margaret. He wants to turn around, but it's too late.)

MARGARET

Hi, Stevie.

STEVIE

Oh, hey.

JEAN

We thought you might be here.

MARGARET

You can sit here if you want.

STEVIE

That's okay, I was just looking / for—

MARGARET

There aren't any seats up front. We looked already.

STEVIE

Oh yeah?

MARGARET

It's fine, sit down. We don't have to be weird.

STEVIE

You sure?

MARGARET

Like you said, you didn't have a choice.

STEVIE

Okay.

MARGARET

Not that I believed that, but sit down anyway. It'll be fun.

(Stevie joins them at the table. Reluctantly.)

DOTTIE

Who's he?

JEAN

Stevie Grimes.

DOTTIE

Suzie's kid?

JEAN

Yeah.

DOTTIE

(Leans over to Stevie) Your mother was a funny bitch. *(Laughing now)* "Who threw that bird at me?!" You know that story?

STEVIE

Yeah.

DOTTIE

So funny: "Who threw that bird at me?!"

MARGARET

He doesn't think it's funny.

DOTTIE

How is that not funny? "Who threw that bird at me?!"

VOICE OF PRIEST

Next game: Inside Square. No B's, No O's. And we're starting with . . . I-17. I . . . 17.

JEAN

Hey Stevie, Karen Finch is telling everyone you're gay.

STEVIE

I heard that.

JEAN

Doesn't that bother you?

STEVIE

Not really.

JEAN

Because you're gay?

STEVIE

No, because I don't care.

VOICE OF PRIEST

G-46.

JEAN

It is peculiar though.

VOICE OF PRIEST

G . . . 46.

JEAN

You coming here all the time?

MARGARET

Leave him alone, Jean.

JEAN

Why? You want me to be nice to the guy that fired you? *(To Dottie)*
She's too nice.

MARGARET

No, I'm not. Mike said I turned mean.

DOTTIE

How were you mean?

JEAN

Who cares? It got her invited to that party, that's all that matters.

VOICE OF PRIEST

N-41. N . . . 41.

STEVIE

(To Jean) So how is coming to bingo peculiar?

MARGARET

Aw, Jesus. See what ya did?

JEAN

Well you don't see too many young guys in here. Bingo's a funny pastime for a young guy.

STEVIE

But not a young *gay* guy?

JEAN

No, you know what I mean.

STEVIE

Not really.

JEAN

Well, look around, there's a bunch of old ladies.

MARGARET

Speak for yourself.

VOICE OF PRIEST

G-58.

JEAN

He knows what I mean.

VOICE OF PRIEST

G . . . 58.

STEVIE

I would if this place was full of gay guys. Is it?

JEAN

No.

STEVIE

Then how is it gay?

JEAN

I don't know.

STEVIE

I'm just trying to win a little money, like everybody else. I don't see how that's gay.

JEAN

Well it is, so I don't know what else to tell ya.

VOICE OF PRIEST

I-21. I . . . 21.

DOTTIE

(Turns to Stevie) Stevie? You want a rabbit?

STEVIE

What?

DOTTIE

I made these rabbits. *(Indicates her wares)*

STEVIE

Oh.

DOTTIE

Five bucks each.

STEVIE

They're nice.

DOTTIE

You want one?

STEVIE

No thank you.

JEAN

Don't like rabbits, Stevie?

DOTTIE

Of course he does. Who doesn't like rabbits?

JEAN

Gay guys.

VOICE OF PRIEST

N-36. N . . . 36.

DOTTIE

I'll give you three for twelve.

STEVIE

I have nowhere to put them.

DOTTIE

Nowhere to put 'em?

STEVIE

I have a lot of clutter in / my—

DOTTIE

They're just little rabbits. "Nowhere to put 'em." You talk like I'm trying to sell you a fridge.

STEVIE

I just don't want them. They're not my taste. I don't care for that sort of thing.

(Silence as Dottie stares at him.)

VOICE OF PRIEST

I-24. I . . . 24.

DOTTIE

I think maybe you *are* gay.

MARGARET

He's not gay. He's dating that Chinese girl up at the store.

STEVIE

She's not Chinese! She's from / *Thailand!*

DOTTIE

What Chinese girl? At the Ho Toy?

MARGARET

I said *store*, not restaurant. The Dollar Store.

DOTTIE

Oh, I thought you meant like Chinese food.

MARGARET

No.

DOTTIE

Like she works at Ho Toy Chinese.

MARGARET

No.

DOTTIE

The Chinese restaurant.

JEAN

No, she works at the Dollar Store! Jesus *Christ*, Dottie!

DOTTIE

Why are you getting mad?

JEAN

Because you're like fuckin' Aunt Clara sometimes! It pisses me off!

DOTTIE

Whose Aunt Clara are you talking about?

JEAN

Nobody's! The show with the witch!

DOTTIE

You don't make any sense, ya know it?

MARGARET

Aren't you glad you sat here, Stevie?

VOICE OF PRIEST

G-60. G . . . 60.

DOTTIE

Hey, you know who else got fired?

JEAN

Who?

DOTTIE

Franny. *(To Stevie)* That's my Russell's wife. Do you know my son Russell? Russell Gillis?

STEVIE

(There's a story here) Yeah, I know Russell Gillis.

VOICE OF PRIEST

N-32.

JEAN

Why'd Franny get fired? She's been at that shop forever.

VOICE OF PRIEST

N . . . 32.

DOTTIE

I guess she got to talking to one of the customers, and forgot about another one, and left something in somebody's hair too long, and clumps of it fell out, or I don't know, some crazy story.

VOICE OF PRIEST

G-52.

DOTTIE

But I guess the owner got mad, and Franny got mouthy, and so out she went.

VOICE OF PRIEST

G . . . 52.

DOTTIE

So now neither of 'em are workin'. Her *or* Russell, and they got nothin' saved up because of her and those stupid scratch tickets.

JEAN

What are they gonna do?

DOTTIE

I don't know. You hiring at the Dollar Store, Stevie?

STEVIE

No. Jesus. Russell Gillis? No.

MARGARET

Franny does good work though. She can go into any salon. She's got a following now.

VOICE OF PRIEST

I-30.

DOTTIE

What following?

VOICE OF PRIEST

I . . . 30.

DOTTIE

A bunch of cripple old ladies with walkers. They can hardly get to her now. Where are they gonna *follow* her to?

MARGARET

Russell will be okay.

DOTTIE

I don't know, their apartment ain't cheap. I might have to help them out, if it comes to that.

JEAN

Comes to what?

DOTTIE

If things get bad, and they need someplace to live.

MARGARET

That's what I thought.

JEAN

You'd give them Margie's apartment?

DOTTIE

I'm not saying it's gonna *happen*.

MARGARET

Funny, how it comes up just as I'm having trouble paying the rent though.

DOTTIE

That's not how it is.

VOICE OF PRIEST

I-28.

JEAN

Jesus, Dottie.

VOICE OF PRIEST

I . . . 28.

DOTTIE

He's my son. What am I supposed to do, let him go homeless?

JEAN

Hey, fuck you, Dottie.

MARGARET

Easy.

JEAN

No, fuck her. She pretends to be your friend.

DOTTIE

I *am* her friend.

JEAN

Yeah, you're a real pal.

MARGARET

It doesn't matter. Dottie, you're right, Russell's your kid. If he needs a place to / stay—

JEAN

It's gonna be fine, Margie. Something's gonna come up for you. Despite these assholes.

VOICE OF PRIEST

I-22.

JEAN

Something always comes up. You'll be okay.

VOICE OF PRIEST

I . . . 22.

MARGARET

Maybe somebody at Mike's party will have something.

JEAN

That's right. You make an impression. People *like* you. Who knows, you might even find a husband there.

MARGARET

Oh yeah, that's exactly what's gonna happen.

VOICE OF PRIEST

N-45.

JEAN

It *could.*

VOICE OF PRIEST

N . . . 45.

MARGARET

Right. 'Cause what guy can resist a middle-aged lady in an outfit from Goodwill?

JEAN

You'd be surprised.

MARGARET

"Oh you're single *and* rich. How lovely, because I'm up to my tits in credit-card debt."

(Jean laughs.)

"Oh, you *like* that? Good, 'cause I'm also in need of major dental work!"

(A little chuckle from Jean.)

"And did I mention that I come with an adult daughter! Not only is she severely retarded, but she still occasionally pisses the bed . . ."

(And for just a moment, Margaret is overcome with emotion. She stops before she embarrasses herself though. It takes everyone by surprise, especially her. Silence. Then Jean turns to Stevie.)

JEAN

See what you did?

VOICE OF PRIEST

G-47.

(Margaret's cell phone starts to ring. She rummages in her bag for it.)

MARGARET

That's my phone.

VOICE OF PRIEST

G . . . 47.

MARGARET

It might be Ruthie. I gave her this number in case something happened to— *(Answers phone)* Hello? . . . Yeah . . . Oh, hi. *(Whispers to Jean)* Do my cards.

(Jean watches Margaret's bingo cards for her.)

(Into the phone) What's goin' on? . . . Uh-huh . . . No, I'm here with Jean.

DOTTIE

(Whispers to Jean) Who's she talking to?

JEAN

Mind your business, Dottie.

MARGARET

(Into phone, confused and disappointed) Uh-huh . . . Oh. Why, what happened?

DOTTIE

(Again to Jean) Something happened.

MARGARET

(Into phone) Is she okay? . . . No, of course . . . Is she okay, though? . . . All right . . . No, it can come on quick like that. If she's sick there's nothing you can—

DOTTIE

Sounds like somebody's sick. Maybe it's Joyce. *(Whispers to Margaret)* Is it Joyce?

(Margaret gestures that it's not.)

Oh, good.

VOICE OF PRIEST

G-56.

MARGARET

No, you can't have a house full of people if she's throwing up like that . . .

VOICE OF PRIEST

G . . . 56.

MARGARET

No, don't be sorry. Don't be. Your daughter's sick . . . I mean, she *is* sick, right? . . . No, I know, I'm just bustin' balls again. That's how I do . . . Hey, whadaya gonna do . . . Yeah, if you reschedule let me know . . . No, I'm saying if you *do*. Okay. Bye.

VOICE OF PRIEST

N-40. N . . . 40.

(Margaret hangs up. She goes back to her bingo cards.)

JEAN

Everything okay?

MARGARET

I just got uninvited.

DOTTIE

To what?

MARGARET

Mike's party. He said it's canceled. I guess his kid's sick.

JEAN

So? It's not the *kid's* party.

MARGARET

I'm just telling you what he said.

VOICE OF PRIEST

I-19. I . . . 19.

JEAN

You think he's lying?

MARGARET

Oh yeah.

JEAN

How do you know?

MARGARET

I could just tell. His voice. He chickened out, he doesn't want me there.

JEAN

Didn't I say he was an asshole?

DOTTIE

You think his wife made him do it?

MARGARET

How should I know?

DOTTIE

I bet he told her you went out.

JEAN

I bet he didn't.

MARGARET

I'm gonna go anyway.

DOTTIE

What?

MARGARET

I'm gonna go to that party.

JEAN

(Smiles) You are?

MARGARET

You think I shouldn't?

JEAN

No, I think you *should*. You *definitely* should.

DOTTIE

Don't take advice from *her*, Margie. She likes trouble.

MARGARET

He said his friends might have something for me. He said that. I think it's rude. To invite someone like that, and then say it's canceled. That's rude.

JEAN

It *is* rude.

VOICE OF PRIEST

N-33.

MARGARET

Besides, I really wanna see that house.

STEVIE

(Raises his hand) Bingo!

JEAN

Cocksucker!

(Lights out.)

Act Two

———

Scene 1

Lights up on a beautiful home. Tasteful and suburban. The living room takes up most of the space. Up and left we may see part of a foyer that leads to the front door. Doorways and corridors lead off to other parts of the house—the kitchen, the dining room, maybe we see a staircase that leads up to the bedrooms. It's a beautifully decorated space. Obviously people with money live here.

It's early evening, say around seven or so. Mike is reading the newspaper when Kate enters with her datebook open. Kate is attractive, pleasant, African American, early thirties.

KATE

What about next Thursday?

MIKE

I can't do Thursday.

KATE

Friday then.

MIKE

You know what my Fridays are like, Katie.

KATE

Well she leaves for Saint Barts on the 12th and she really wants to meet before that.

MIKE

Of course she does. That's how she pays for these trips to Saint Barts. We miss a couple sessions, and she might not be able to swing the bar tab.

KATE

What about Tuesday morning? Can you go in late?

MIKE

Aren't we done?

KATE

No, Michael, she thinks it's important that / we keep—

MIKE

No, I know she does, but that's what they do. They string you along forever, and make you think you need their counsel—

KATE

We *do* need her counsel.

MIKE

Yes, and we got it. For many months. But are we learning anything *new*? Every week we go in / there—

KATE

I know.

MIKE

She says the same stuff, and then we say the same stuff, and then we write her another check.

KATE

I know.

MIKE

It's become this security blanket.

KATE

Well maybe I *need* a security blanket.

MIKE

(Beat) Okay. If you want to keep going to her, I'm fine with that. I just thought I'd bring it up. I'm fine either way. I can go in late on Tuesday if that's what you wanna do.

KATE

That's what I want to do.

MIKE

Okay. Do you notice how quiet Ally is?

KATE

I do.

MIKE

What'd I tell ya?

KATE

She's asleep?

MIKE

The Benadryl knocked her out.

KATE

You put the basin beside the bed?

MIKE

Yeah.

KATE

And changed the comforter?

MIKE

For what?

KATE

I didn't want her puking on that new duvet.

MIKE

I forgot. I can go switch / them— *(Moves to go)*

KATE

Well don't do it now, you'll wake her up.

MIKE

You don't want me to change it?

KATE

No, I want her to sleep. I just wish you had changed it while I had her in the tub.

MIKE

I'll do it now.

KATE

Michael—

MIKE

It'll take me one minute. I won't wake her up.

(He heads upstairs. The doorbell rings.)

There they are. I told you they'd come.

KATE

If you wake her up, we'll never get her back down.

MIKE

I won't wake her up.

(He's gone upstairs. Kate crosses to the foyer to open the front door.)

MARGARET

(Off) Hello.

KATE

(Off) Hi.

MARGARET

(Off) I'm Margaret.

KATE

(Off) Hi Margaret, come on in.

(Margaret enters the foyer.)

MARGARET

I didn't know if I was supposed to use the side door or the front door, or what I was supposed / to do.

KATE

I told Wally the side door, but it doesn't matter. It's just easier with the driveway right there, but this is fine.

(They move into the living room.)

MARGARET

Am I early?

KATE

Not at all. I thought you'd be here sooner actually. You all must be busy.

MARGARET

Not really.

KATE

Oh. Okay. Well the kitchen's this way. Did you bring anyone with you?

MARGARET

No. I threatened to though. *(Chuckles)* Did he mention that? I was gonna bring the Feeneys.

KATE

I'm sorry?

MARGARET

No, I didn't bring anyone.

KATE

(Stops) You're not going to carry this stuff yourself, I hope?

MARGARET

What stuff?

KATE

The glasses, and the— It's pretty heavy. There are some folding tables that have to go, too. Wally usually sends a couple guys to pick it all up.

MARGARET

Oh yeah?

(Margaret stares at her, confused. There's obviously been a mix-up.)

KATE

You're not with the caterers.

MARGARET

No.

KATE

Oh my god. I am so sorry.

MARGARET

That's okay.

KATE

(Laughing now) I can't believe I did that.

MARGARET

I was wondering why you kept saying Wally.

KATE

I'm sorry.

MARGARET

I'm like, "Who the hell's Wally?"

KATE

(Laughing) I just assumed he sent one of the waitresses. Which doesn't even make sense really, but it's been so crazy here today.

MARGARET

That's all right.

111

KATE

(Still laughing) I just escort you right in without—

MARGARET

Mike invited me. I'm Margaret. *(Off her blank look)* Margie Walsh? From Southie?

KATE

(Realizing) Jesus. Oh my god, I am so sorry.

MARGARET

It's okay.

KATE

You must think I'm a crazy person.

MARGARET

It's fine.

KATE

It didn't even occur to me that you might be here for the party.

MARGARET

Am I the first? I should've come a little later.

KATE

Did Michael not call you?

MARGARET

No, he did, / but—

KATE

We canceled. We canceled the party last night.

MARGARET

(Beat) Oh.

112

KATE

Yeah, Michael was supposed to call you. Our daughter got sick /
so—

MARGARET

Oh my god.

KATE

That's why I thought you were with the caterer. They dropped off
a bunch of stuff yesterday, and then we canceled last night, so they
said they'd send someone to pick things up.

MARGARET

You canceled.

KATE

Michael said he called everyone / but—

MARGARET

No, he did, but— I misunderstood.

KATE

Oh.

MARGARET

I didn't understand what he was—

KATE

It was probably the way he said it.

MARGARET

Yeah.

KATE

He does the same thing to me all the time.

113

(Mike comes downstairs.)

MIKE

Mission accomplished. I was like a magician with a table cloth.

(Mike enters the living room. Silence as he takes in Margaret.)

MARGARET

Hello.

KATE

Margaret didn't get your message.

MARGARET

No, I got it, I just misunderstood it.

MIKE

You did?

KATE

He can be so confusing sometimes.

MARGARET

No, it's my fault, I wasn't / listening or—

KATE

Honestly, don't worry about it.

MARGARET

I feel so stupid.

KATE

Why don't you take off your coat?

MARGARET

No, I'm gonna go.

KATE

Don't be ridiculous.

MARGARET

No, there's no party, your daughter's sick—

KATE

She's asleep now. Let me take your coat.

MARGARET

That's okay.

KATE

Come on, you're here now, you might as well have a quick glass of wine.

MARGARET

No, you don't have to do that.

KATE

We're just about to open a bottle.

MARGARET

Still, I feel dumb, barging in / when—

KATE

We were just sitting here waiting for the caterers to pick / up the—

MARGARET

I know, but—

KATE

One drink. You can have *one* drink.

MIKE

Well don't force her, Kate. If she doesn't / want to—

KATE

I'm not forcing her, I'm just saying if she drove all this way—

MARGARET

I took the T.

KATE

You took the T?

MARGARET

Yeah.

KATE

No, you have to stay then.

MIKE

You don't *have* to.

KATE

But we would *like* you to.

(Pause. Margaret finally relents.)

MARGARET

Okay, but only for a minute.

MIKE

There ya go.

KATE

Let me take your coat.

(Margaret unbuttons her coat. Kate glances at the coat, but doesn't betray what she thinks of it. She just brings it to the hall closet to hang up.
Margaret wears the nicest dress she could afford.)

MARGARET

This is so stupid. I don't know how I did this.

KATE

Stop. It's fine. Have a seat, don't be shy.

MIKE

Oh she's not shy, are ya, Margie.

MARGARET

She thought I was with the caterer.

MIKE

She what?

KATE

They were supposed to come pick up the tables, that's why I /
thought—

MARGARET

It's okay.

KATE

If it's any consolation, people always think I'm the *nanny*, so . . .

MARGARET

(Beat) The nanny?

KATE

If I'm out with Ally, or at the park? They assume I'm her nanny.
Because she's so white.

MARGARET

I see.

KATE

I actually had a woman offer me a job. She said, "I don't know if you're looking for a new family, but we pay really well." Oh, it made me so mad.

MARGARET

I bet.

KATE

(Beat) I'm sorry, Margaret.

MARGARET

No, you were expecting the caterers. Who else is gonna ring the bell?

KATE

Anyway, you settle in, I'm gonna get some cheese together.

MARGARET

You don't have to do that.

KATE

I do actually. I was able to cancel the caterers, but the cheese guy was a complete ass. He wouldn't take anything back.

MIKE

The fridge is packed with the stuff.

KATE

You're not lactose intolerant, I hope.

MARGARET

I don't think so.

KATE

Oh good, because all day I've been saying, "What are we gonna do with all this cheese?!" You ringing that bell was the best thing to happen to us.

MARGARET

Oh yeah?

KATE

Now you're trapped here until that cheese is *gone*.

MARGARET

(A polite laugh) Okay.

KATE

I'll be right back. Michael, get her some wine.

(Kate heads off into the kitchen. Margaret and Mike are left alone.)

MIKE

We have beer if you'd rather have beer.

MARGARET

(Beat) Wine is fine.

MIKE

Red?

MARGARET

Sure.

(He goes to the glassware cabinet and gets a wine glass, opens a bottle and pours her some wine over the following:)

I'm sorry, Mike. I misunderstood.

MIKE

How do you mean?

MARGARET

About the party. I didn't realize / that—

MIKE

Right, I'm not sure how you could've done that.

MARGARET

I know.

MIKE

I thought I was pretty clear when we talked.

MARGARET

No, I know.

MIKE

I said Ally was sick, and so my wife wanted to cancel.

MARGARET

I thought you were lying though.

MIKE

(Beat) Ah.

MARGARET

I thought you were just making up an excuse / to—

MIKE

Why would I lie?

MARGARET

I don't know. I just thought you didn't want me to come. It seemed suspicious. To cancel at the last minute like that.

MIKE

Ally got sick. Kate thought it'd be better if we called it off.

MARGARET

No, I know that *now.*

MIKE

You're paranoid.

(He hands her the wine. Margaret looks around a bit.)

So you found it okay.

MARGARET

No problem. That receptionist of yours gives good directions.

MIKE

I'll let her know.

MARGARET

I was early though, so I walked around the block a few times.

MIKE

And you lived to tell the tale.

MARGARET

I should've figured out there was no party. Your driveway was empty. Most of your lights were off.

MIKE

Yeah, well.

MARGARET

The house is beautiful.

MIKE

Thanks.

MARGARET

I knew it would be. *(Beat)* I pictured pillars though.

MIKE

Pillars?

MARGARET

On the outside? Like columns?

MIKE

Like Tara?

MARGARET

Tara?

MIKE

Gone with the Wind?

MARGARET

I don't know, I guess. Yeah.

MIKE

That's funny.

MARGARET

It's still nice though.

MIKE

But you would've preferred pillars.

MARGARET

I don't know.

(They drink.)

Should I go?

MIKE

No, you can't go now, Kate's getting cheese. You can't leave when she's getting cheese. She'll think I chased you off. *(Beat)* Besides, she wanted to meet you.

MARGARET

(Beat) She did?

MIKE

Yeah, she doesn't believe I grew up in Southie. You're my evidence.

MARGARET

Oh.

MIKE

You'll have to tell her what a hoodlum I was.

MARGARET

What do you mean?

MIKE

She only knows me as Mr. Doctor-Man.

MARGARET

Oh, I see.

MIKE

You gotta set her straight.

MARGARET

You want me to mention the Irish mob? How you ran with Whitey Bulger? How many bodies should I tell her you buried?

MIKE

All right. If you're gonna make fun / of me—

MARGARET

Well, I don't know what you told her.

MIKE

I didn't *lie* to her.

MARGARET

Well, you said hoodlum.

MIKE

You know what I meant.

MARGARET

You were just a kid from the projects.

MIKE

Exactly.

MARGARET

So that means hoodlum?

MIKE

No. I didn't mean to say it like that. Forget it. How's the wine?

MARGARET

How the fuck should I know?

(Silence as they drink.)

What'd you tell her about me?

MIKE

I just said you might come to the party.

MARGARET

(Beat) That's not very interesting. You must've said *something* else. Otherwise why would she want to meet me?

MIKE

No, just that we ran in the same crowd when we were kids. And how you came by the office.

MARGARET

Looking for work.

MIKE

Yeah.

MARGARET

Okay. *(Beat)* You didn't mention we used to go out?

MIKE

Oh god no. No, I didn't men— No.

MARGARET

How come?

MIKE

I don't know. That was such a blip.

MARGARET

Huh.

MIKE

A couple months.

MARGARET

No, I know.

MIKE

We were friends for so long before that. I just said we were friends.

MARGARET

(A little chuckle) Okay. So she won't be weird about me at all?

MIKE

No.

MARGARET

Good.

MIKE

I mean, so long as you don't mention it.

MARGARET

(Beat) Okay.

MIKE

I just said we were friends.

MARGARET

Right.

(Pause as they drink.)

MARGARET

So she *might* get weird? If she knew?

MIKE

No. I don't think so. *(Beat)* I don't know. It's just . . . we're in a really good place right now, and I don't wanna . . .

MARGARET

Stir anything up?

MIKE

Exactly.

MARGARET

(Beat. Smiles) What'd you do?

MIKE

Nothing.

MARGARET

"We're in a really good place right now."

MIKE

We *are*.

MARGARET

Which means at some point you *weren't*.

MIKE

Margaret—

MARGARET

What'd you do?

MIKE

Nothing.

MARGARET

It involves that Dominican receptionist doesn't it?

MIKE

Jesus. No.

MARGARET

(Laughs) I'm just bustin' balls.

127

MIKE

Can you just . . . not mention we dated?

MARGARET

All right.

MIKE

We were practically kids after all.

MARGARET

I'm not the one making a big deal out of it.

MIKE

I'm not making a big deal, I just wanna . . .

MARGARET

Keep it secret.

MIKE

Well don't make it sound *dirty*.

MARGARET

You did that, not me.

(Kate comes in with a tray loaded with cheeses and crackers.)

KATE

Okay, here we go.

MIKE

Wow. That's a lot of cheese, Katie.

MARGARET

Look at that.

KATE

And this is only half of them. There's plenty more if you don't find what you like.

MARGARET

You can smell them.

KATE

Yeah, some of them are pretty pungent. I try not to inhale.

MIKE

The worse the smell the better the cheese.

KATE

(Places cheese down) What do you like, Margaret?

MARGARET

Oh, I don't know. Which one's the Cracker Barrel? *(Off Kate's look)* I'm kidding.

KATE

(Laughs) Oh, good! I was afraid you were seri— *(Catches herself)* Not that there's anything wrong with— I actually love Cracker Barrel. I lived on it in grad school.

MIKE

Okay, you can stop.

KATE

What, I *did*.

MARGARET

I'm sure these are all great. You wanna gimme a tour?

KATE

A tour?

MARGARET

Of the cheese?

KATE

Oh, I thought you meant the house.

MARGARET

That'd be nice too, but I meant the cheese. I don't know what's what.

MIKE

You don't want a cheese tour.

MARGARET

Sure I do. *(Indicates cheese)* What's this one?

KATE

Um, that's Humboldt Fog, which is a goat. Cheese.

MARGARET

Okay, and this one?

KATE

Epoisses. Which is a French cow's milk. It's very good. If you want something a little / nutty—

MARGARET

(Smelling Epoisses) Whoa. You got anything mild?

MIKE

(Indicates a cheese) Do this one, Margie.

KATE

That's Wensleydale. *(Cuts her a piece)*

MIKE

She's not gonna remember the names.

KATE

How do you know? Just because *you* can't remember them /
doesn't mean—

MIKE

(To Margaret) Let me give you *my* tour.

KATE

Here we go.

MIKE

(Indicates cheeses) That's Creamy Drippy, that's Smells Like Ammonia,
that's Body Odor . . .

KATE

This is what he does.

MIKE

That's Close to Cheddar but Not As Good, that one is Moldy
Basement . . .

KATE

This is how he orders at the cheese shop, too.

MIKE

They think it's funny.

KATE

No they don't.

MIKE

"A wedge of Moldy Basement, please."

131

KATE

They don't think that's funny, Michael.

MIKE

Yes they do.

KATE

I think they're slightly offended actually.

MIKE

You're crazy. They love me in there.

KATE

I don't think they do.

MARGARET

(Eating cheese) This one's very good.

KATE

Wensleydale.

MARGARET

Wensleydale. Good to know.

KATE

(To Mike) Guess I get to throw you a party after all. *(To Margaret)* He was adamant we cancel when Ally got sick.

MARGARET

(Beat) He was?

MIKE

No, we *both* were. We discussed it.

MARGARET

Huh.

132

KATE

I said she would've been perfectly fine with the babysitter and a DVD upstairs, / but—

MIKE

Kate, come on—

KATE

No, you were right, I know. I'm bad. *(To Margaret)* It killed me to cancel. I *love* to throw parties. Just like my mama. You can take the girl out of Georgetown but you can't take Georgetown out of the girl.

MARGARET

We say that in Southie, too! "You can take the girl out of Southie / but . . ."

KATE

Oh yeah.

MARGARET

Same thing.

KATE

Same thing.

(They all eat cheese.)

MARGARET

So how'd you meet?

KATE

My father introduced us.

MARGARET

Really.

KATE

Michael worked under him at GU Hospital in D.C.

MARGARET

Huh. The boss's daughter.

MIKE

It was an arranged marriage.

KATE

(Laughs) It *was*, practically. The way he kept dragging you out for those barbecues? "Katie, you remember, Michael."

MIKE

He was a wise man.

KATE

Yeah, the jury's still out on that one. I think he was just sick of me bringing home puppeteers. And djembe players.

MIKE

(Chuckles) Djembe players.

MARGARET

Is that a sports thing?

KATE

It's a drum.

MARGARET

I see. Well you did good then. You don't wanna marry the drummer.

KATE

No, I guess not.

(Margaret takes them in for a moment.)

134

MARGARET

Oh I just remembered! I brought you something! *(Heads to coat closet)* It's with my coat.

MIKE

You brought me something?

MARGARET

Yeah, just a little gifty for your birthday.

KATE

That is so nice.

MARGARET

Don't get too excited, it's just . . . nothing big.

(She returns with a plastic bag, which she hands to Mike.)

I probably should've wrapped it, but I didn't have any paper in the house.

(Mike pulls one of Dottie's rabbits out of the bag.)

MIKE

Ohhh . . .

KATE

Look at that.

MIKE

Is that a rabbit?

MARGARET

My landlady made it.

KATE

That is so cute.

MARGARET

I thought your daughter might like it.

MIKE

She definitely will. Thank you.

KATE

The eyes move.

MIKE

I saw that.

MARGARET

Never come to a party empty handed. Isn't that what they say?

MIKE

We'll have to find a spot for that.

KATE

Right over here.

(Kate takes the rabbit and puts it in a prominent spot on a bookshelf.)

MARGARET

The head's a little lopsided.

MIKE

No, it looks nice.

MARGARET

You like it?

KATE

It's very cute.

MARGARET

My friend Jeannie hates those things.

MIKE

No, it's cute. Ally's gonna love it. We'll show her in the morning. Thank you.

(They eat cheese.)

KATE

So, are you going to tell me all of Michael's secrets?

MARGARET

You bet.

MIKE

Uh-oh.

KATE

You were in the same class?

MARGARET

No. I repeated a grade, and he skipped a grade. So he got ahead of me. Smarty.

KATE

(To Mike) You never told me you skipped a grade. *(Back to Margaret)* He hardly tells me anything. You know, he's met all of my childhood friends, and I've met *none* of his.

MIKE

Yes, you have.

KATE

Not *one*.

MIKE

What about my groomsmen? Dean and Omar / and—

KATE

College buddies. I'm not talking / about—

MIKE

They're the ones with the secrets!

KATE

No, I'm talking about somebody who knows the true story.

MARGARET

What true story?

KATE

All of it. The stuff he tells me, I think he's making half of it up.

MIKE

(To Margaret) See? What'd I tell you? My own wife thinks I'm a compulsive liar.

KATE

Well, it's not like you don't have a history.

MIKE

Hey, easy.

KATE

(Chuckles) I'm sorry. That'll come up in the next session.

MIKE

Seriously, Katie.

KATE

What, I'm joking. *(To Margaret)* Really though, you have to be my bullshit meter, because when he talks about growing up, he makes himself out to be this *Upton Sinclair* character.

MARGARET

I don't know what that means.

MIKE

Nobody does, Margie. Don't listen to her. *(To Kate)* What are you—?

KATE

What.

MIKE

Upton Sinclair. *(To Margaret)* Kate teaches literature.

MARGARET

Oh, wow.

MIKE

Novels, and . . .

MARGARET

Yeah, I know what literature is.

KATE

I teach at BU.

MARGARET

Harvard wasn't interested?

KATE

(Beat) What?

MARGARET

I'm just kidding. That's great.

MIKE

(To Kate) Ya see what she did there? She zotzed you a little bit.

KATE

I know.

MARGARET

I was kidding.

MIKE

"Harvard wasn't interested?"

KATE

It was like my mother was here for a second.

MARGARET

They hiring over there?

KATE

At Harvard?

MARGARET

No, BU. I'm talking about myself now.

KATE

Oh.

MARGARET

Didn't Mike tell you I was / looking—

KATE

Looking for work, yeah, he said. Um, no I don't know. You'd have to go to personnel, I guess. I don't know how that works.

MARGARET

That's why I came to the party. Mike said one of his friends might have something.

KATE

He did?

MIKE

That's not exactly what I / said—

KATE

He said a friend had a job?

MIKE

Not a specific friend. Just . . . *someone* might— She said if she mingled, could she ask around.

MARGARET

But of course nobody's here. Which is why I was asking about BU.

KATE

I see.

MARGARET

So, who's Upton Whatever?

KATE

He's a writer. He wrote about . . . you know, the city . . .

MARGARET

Poor people?

MIKE

Upton Sinclair's a bad comparison.

141

KATE

Not the way *you* talk. You make it sound so dire. With the violence and drugs and rats—

MARGARET

(Chuckles) Oh, the rats. What've you been telling her?

MIKE

Just that it was rough. It was a rough neighborhood.

MARGARET

It wasn't *that* rough.

MIKE

You didn't live in Old Harbor. The projects were a little rougher.

MARGARET

You had a nice apartment.

MIKE

My mother *kept* it nice, but still—

MARGARET

She *did* keep it nice. That's probably where you got those lace-curtain ideas.

MIKE

(To Kate) See? Lace-curtain?

MARGARET

He told you about that?

KATE

You hit a nerve.

MIKE

Well you mentioning Upton Sinclair doesn't help my argument.

MARGARET

You lost the argument when the cheese came out.

KATE

Oh I hope not.

MARGARET

You want Mike's big secret? Here it is: he didn't have it so bad.

MIKE

Come on, Margaret.

MARGARET

Not compared to other people.

MIKE

The way my father worked?

MARGARET

Let's start with the fact that you *had* a father, and he *worked*.

MIKE

The clothes from Morgan Memorial? The food stamps? The Welly Cheese?

MARGARET

You seemed like a pretty happy kid. You have some nice memories.

MIKE

Of course I do / but—

MARGARET

You obviously like to reminisce. So it couldn't have been *too* bad. Least you managed to get out.

MIKE

Because I worked my ass off. That's the only way out of there.

MARGARET

(Beat) Right.

MIKE

I didn't mean *you* don't work your ass off.

MARGARET

No?

MIKE

Obviously you work hard.

MARGARET

Hey, thanks.

MIKE

Don't take it the wrong way. I was talking about scholarships and what / I had to—

MARGARET

No, you worked hard, you're right. You escaped. I didn't. *(Beat)* You had a little help, but you did it.

MIKE

What does that mean? What help did I get?

MARGARET

You were luckier than most people, that's all. You were smart. You had a dad that pushed you. You had some advantages. So I don't know if I'd be complaining if / I were you.

MIKE

I'm not complaining, I just said we struggled. Which we did. Life wasn't easy.

MARGARET

Of course not. So? That's normal. To struggle. For *most* people, it's normal. Most people *I* know at least. That's just how it is. Just because we weren't comfortable doesn't mean we were *miserable*. *(A little laugh)* I mean, I am *now*, but . . . Back then wasn't so bad, Mikey.

(Silence.)

KATE

We can find a job for her, can't we? Somebody has to have a job for her.

MIKE

Like who?

KATE

What about Tom? He's gotta have something down / at the—

MIKE

Tom just laid off half his staff.

KATE

Well Bernie then?

MIKE

At the lab? How is she gonna work at a lab?

KATE

I'm gonna think of something for you, Margaret. Now I got my thinking cap on.

MARGARET

Okay.

KATE

The wheels are turning.

MARGARET

Great.

KATE

But in return you have to tell me some Mike stories.

MARGARET

Okay.

MIKE

Oh, I don't think I like that deal.

KATE

He said he got into fights.

MARGARET

What fights?

MIKE

Just . . . schoolyard stuff. Or up at the Boys Club.

MARGARET

With who?

MIKE

Everybody. Danny Turpin, Dominic Vecchi . . .

MARGARET

The only fight I remember was in the Old Harbor courtyard.

146

MIKE

Oh, that was— You don't remember the thing with Danny Turpin?

MARGARET

No, I remember Old Harbor. Right down your way. And even that didn't really count.

KATE

Why didn't it count?

MARGARET

He was just trying to prove something. He was trying to be one of the hard guys.

MIKE

Come on—

MARGARET

You *were*. It was you and Marty McDermott, and Gobie jumped in, and the Burke brothers . . . Who else?

MIKE

It was so long ago, I don't—

MARGARET

Johnny Dugger was there I think. You were all playing basketball.

MIKE

You know, that Danny Turpin story is pretty funny—

MARGARET

And we were on the front stoop watching. Me and Jeannie. Suzie Grimes and Sheila Sheen. Remember her? She was a whore, huh? Pardon my French.

147

                    KATE

Was this a gang fight?

                    MARGARET

(Chuckles) Gang fight. No. Some kids came over from Columbia
Point.

                    MIKE

Come on, Margaret—

                    MARGARET

Old Harbor was right on the Dot border, so Columbia Point was
like right there. I don't know what they were thinking / but—

                    MIKE

One of 'em threw a bottle.

                    KATE

Who did?

                    MIKE

One of the kids. One of the guys from Columbia Point. That's
how it started.

                    MARGARET

I don't remember that.

                    MIKE

Yeah, it almost hit Marty. That's what started the whole thing.

                    MARGARET

Huh.

                    MIKE

One of them chucked a bottle, and so we chased them off.

MARGARET

(To Kate) Except one of the kids fell, running away, and smashed his face into a mailbox. His friends kept running, and Mike beat the shit out of him. Pardon my French.

MIKE

Not just me.

MARGARET

No, everybody did. They all—

KATE

They beat him up?

MARGARET

Yeah. It was a mess. His face was . . . I was scared. We all were, I think.

MIKE

He chucked a bottle.

KATE

Still. Six guys on one.

MIKE

It wasn't six.

MARGARET

I think it was. At least six. I think I'm forgetting a couple people. If your father hadn't come out to break it up, I don't know what would've happened.

KATE

Jesus.

MARGARET

(Beat) You wanted to hear about fights.

KATE

That's not a *fight.*

MARGARET

No, you're right. It wasn't much of a fight.

(Silence.)

MIKE

(Off Kate's look) What. Everyone's an idiot when they're seventeen.

KATE

(Referring to her wine) Does this taste corked to you? A little bit?

MARGARET

I don't know.

KATE

Something tastes . . . I don't think I like this. I'm gonna switch to white. Would you rather have white, Margaret?

MARGARET

Doesn't matter.

KATE

I'm gonna get some white.

(The side doorbell rings.)

And that's the caterers picking up.

MARGARET

Are ya sure?

KATE

(A polite chuckle) I'll get confirmation this time.

MARGARET

(To Kate) Good thinkin'.

MIKE

Want me to help deal with them?

KATE

(As she goes) No, I got it.

(Mike and Margaret are left alone. After a moment, Margaret grabs a piece of cheese.)

MARGARET

She seems nice, Mikey.

MIKE

She *is* nice.

MARGARET

Gonna put her thinking cap on for me.

MIKE

She's got a big heart.

MARGARET

I can tell. *(Beat)* And she's black.

MIKE

(Beat) Yes. That is true. She is black. *(Beat)* You seemed surprised by that.

MARGARET

No, I don't care. I was just saying.

MIKE

You did seem surprised though.

MARGARET

When?

MIKE

Back in the office. When I showed you the photo.

MARGARET

Oh, no that / wasn't—

MIKE

Your eyebrows went up.

MARGARET

Because she was so young.

MIKE

Okay.

MARGARET

I was like, "Holy shit, she's so young." Not 'cause she was black.

MIKE

All right. My mistake.

(They drink in silence for a couple beats.)

Why did you tell her that story?

MARGARET

She was begging me for a fight story.

MIKE

She wasn't begging.

152

MARGARET

(Chuckles) I think she was expecting something out of the Bowery Boys though.

MIKE

Well, you didn't give her that.

MARGARET

You ever hear from any of those guys? From the neighborhood?

MIKE

Not really.

MARGARET

I didn't think so. I bump into Johnny Dugger every once and a while. He owns that variety store down the rotary. He's doing okay. But you know Sheila Sheen's dead, right?

MIKE

No.

MARGARET

Yeah, she OD'd a few years back.

MIKE

That's too bad.

MARGARET

I don't know where the Burkes ended up. Nowhere good, I don't think. Marty McDermott's in prison. And remember his sister Cookie? She was living on the street. She'd sit outside the bank and ask people for money. She died last week. Right on the sidewalk. *My* age.

MIKE

Jesus.

MARGARET

It's good you got out, right?

MIKE

I guess.

MARGARET

(Beat) Do you ever wonder what would've happened if you hadn't though?

MIKE

What do you mean?

MARGARET

If you hadn't left for U-Penn? You think we would've stayed together?

MIKE

Oh. Christ, Margie, let's not do *that*. She's coming right back, and I don't want / her to—

MARGARET

You haven't wondered?

MIKE

That was just a summer thing. Kids have those. I'm sure you had them after me.

MARGARET

Not really.

MIKE

Only because you were with Gobie. You jumped in with him right after I left. That went on, right? For a long time.

MARGARET

It's just something I wondered. If you weren't going off to U-Penn in September, would we have kept going.

MIKE

You broke up with *me*.

MARGARET

I know, because you were going away.

MIKE

You broke up with *me*, Margie.

MARGARET

I *know*! *(Beat)* Remember how pretty I was though?

MIKE

I do.

MARGARET

You thought I was *sooo* pretty. And that was all it took for me to like you back.

MIKE

It wasn't my irresistible charms?

MARGARET

Nope. *(Beat)* You *were* charming though.

(This lingers in the air for a moment.)

MIKE

Anyway. What's done is done. It all worked out.

MARGARET

It did?

155

MIKE

You know what I mean.

MARGARET

Yeah. *(Beat)* Well you made the right choice.

(Kate reenters with two glasses of white wine.)

KATE

(Referring to the caterers) They're taking the stuff out the back. *(Referring to the wine)* This is much better. Margaret, gimme your glass. Switch to this. *(Swaps Margaret's red for the white)* You'll like this better. I prefer white anyway. Which is why I married Michael actually.

MIKE

Wow, that is a / terrible joke.

KATE

I know. I'm just being / stupid.

MARGARET

(Referring to an ornate crystal vase on a bookcase) What is that?

MIKE

The vase?

MARGARET

Is that what that is?

KATE

That was my push present.

MARGARET

Your what?

MIKE

Kate, don't call it / that.

KATE

I know, as soon as I said it, I realized how obnoxious it sounded. *(To Margaret)* It was a gift from Michael, when Ally was born.

MARGARET

Push present?

KATE

That's what *he* called it.

MARGARET

For pushing out the baby?

MIKE

I didn't make up the phrase. A lot of people use it.

MARGARET

I've never heard of that.

KATE

Obviously the baby was gift enough, but it *was* nice after twenty hours of labor.

MARGARET

He gave you a vase?

MIKE

I know, it's gross. *(To Kate)* Why did you tell her that?

KATE

She asked what it was. *(To Margaret)* A lot of husbands do it.

MARGARET

Give push presents?

KATE

Usually it's *jewelry*, but yeah.

MARGARET

I never heard of that. It's nice. *(Beat)* I'd be a nervous wreck though, having something that nice with a kid in the house.

KATE

Oh, she knows not to touch it. And it's insured anyway.

MARGARET

Oh. Good.

(Silence.)

KATE

Do you have any children?

MARGARET

I have a daughter. She's a grown-up though.

KATE

Oh yeah? And what does *she* do?

MARGARET

Not a lot.

(An awkward pause.)

KATE

But you like kids?

MARGARET

Sure. I mean, I don't want to be a grandmother or / anything, but—

KATE

Because I was thinking, if you really need work, we're always looking for someone to watch Ally. For when we go out. Michael's always got these events he's dragging me to. Dinners and . . . auctions, or whatever.

(Pause as Margaret and Mike both look to her.)

MARGARET

You want me to babysit?

KATE

It's not a full-time job obviously, but it's something. At least a few times a month. How much are we paying Sarah now?

MIKE

I don't know.

KATE

We just gave her a raise last month. She's up to fifteen dollars, I think.

MARGARET

For babysitting?

KATE

It's not a lot but—

MARGARET

Fifteen dollars an hour?

KATE

Not a lot of hours. I mean, but if you can't find something it would at least give you a little money.

MIKE

Wait a minute.

KATE

What.

MIKE

You can't just fire Sarah.

KATE

It wouldn't be *firing* her, she's not on *salary*. She's a babysitter.

MIKE

Still.

KATE

And it's not like she needs the money.

MIKE

How do you know she doesn't?

KATE

She drives a Beemer.

MIKE

That's not hers.

KATE

Yes it is. It's *her* car.

MIKE

That her father bought. She didn't buy it with her own money.

KATE

Why are you arguing? You honestly think Sarah Katzman needs the money more than Margaret?

MIKE

Of course not.

KATE

All right then.

MIKE

But Margaret can't work nights.

KATE

Oh.

MIKE

Isn't that what you said? When I mentioned the cleaning crew?

MARGARET

You said you couldn't get me a job with the cleaning crew.

MIKE

No, I couldn't, but when it came up you said you couldn't work nights.

MARGARET

Well, they wouldn't have paid me fifteen dollars an hour. For fifteen dollars I can work nights.

MIKE

How? You pay someone to watch Joyce while you watch Ally? That's a wash.

MARGARET

No it isn't. I don't pay my babysitter no fifteen bucks an hour. Trust me, I'd definitely come out ahead.

KATE

Who's Joyce?

MARGARET

Joyce is my daughter. She was born premature.

KATE

Oh.

(This really confuses Kate.)

MIKE

The thing is, Ally knows Sarah, and she's comfortable with her. We can't just change everything up. That's not fair to Ally.

MARGARET

I see.

KATE

Ally won't care. She sees Sarah for half an hour, and then it's time for bed. Ally hardly *sees* Sarah.

MIKE

But she *knows* her. She doesn't know Margaret.

KATE

So we'll introduce them.

MIKE

This isn't about you, Margie.

MARGARET

No?

MIKE

It's about Ally, and what she's used to.

162

KATE

Ally's asleep the whole time. Sarah just sits down here and reads. You talk like they're best friends.

MIKE

Come on, Katie, this is— Margaret doesn't want our charity.

MARGARET

Sure, I do.

KATE

It's not charity, it's a job.

MIKE

Plus Sarah is CPR certified, and she knows all the phone numbers god forbid something goes wrong.

KATE

What phone numbers?

MIKE

The pediatrician, poison control—

KATE

Those numbers are on the fridge, Michael!

MIKE

I know but—

KATE

They're all on the fridge!

MARGARET

He doesn't want me to babysit.

163

MIKE

No, that's not it.

MARGARET

He wouldn't feel comfortable.

MIKE

Not just me. Ally wouldn't. Ally knows Sarah.

KATE

You're ridiculous, you know it? It's just a couple times a month.

MIKE

What about the Foleys? Aren't they always looking for a babysitter?

KATE

I'm not gonna send her to the *Foleys*.

MIKE

Why not?

KATE

They're lunatics.

MARGARET

How much do *they* pay?

KATE

You say you want to help her. "Hey, come to my house, Margaret. I'll introduce you to my buddies."

MIKE

That's not what I said.

KATE

"Lemme find you a job."

MIKE

That's not what I said.

MARGARET

Yes it is.

MIKE

Margaret—

MARGARET

That's what you said.

MIKE

No, that's what you *heard*.

MARGARET

Oh, okay.

MIKE

It's not what I said, it's what you heard. Just like I *said* the party was canceled, and you *heard* that it wasn't.

MARGARET

(To Kate) Well so much for your thinking cap.

KATE

I still don't understand what the problem is.

MARGARET

He obviously doesn't want me working here.

MIKE

Don't say it like that.

MARGARET

Well do you? Do you or don't you?

165

MIKE

(Beat) No, I don't.

MARGARET

There. End of discussion.

KATE

No, he doesn't get to decide / what—

MARGARET

No, I understand. You can't force him. He thinks Ally wouldn't feel safe with me watching her.

MIKE

I didn't say safe, Margie, I said *comfortable*. And I don't have to justify why I don't want you watching my child.

MARGARET

No, you don't, because it's obvious. I'm not babysitter material.

MIKE

Margaret—

MARGARET

I'm not smart enough to watch a kid sleep.

MIKE

It's not just—

MARGARET

I don't know the right things. Or how to use a phone—

MIKE

Okay—

MARGARET

—and I might also be a racist.

MIKE

Now come on, nobody said you were a / racist.

MARGARET

You might as well have *(Turns to Kate)* I mentioned you were black, so—

KATE

How does that make you racist?

MARGARET

Ask him.

MIKE

It doesn't!

MARGARET

All I know, is that I'm not the one who chased down that boy at the Old Harbor Projects.

MIKE

(Beat) All right, now you're just causing / trouble.

KATE

What boy?

MARGARET

The one we talked about. That's the part he didn't mention.

MIKE

What does this have to do / with—?

MARGARET

Nobody threw a bottle. That fight he was talking about, in the courtyard? Nobody threw a bottle at anybody. Those kids came over from Columbia Point, which was a *black* part of Dorchester. That's the part he didn't mention.

MIKE

Because it wasn't relevant.

MARGARET

Oh, is that why?

MIKE

Yes.

MARGARET

There was no bottle. Marty McDermott saw those kids and yelled, "What are those niggers doing over here?" and that's when everybody went running.

MIKE

Look, you're obviously trying to bait my wife.

MARGARET

I'm *what*?

MIKE

Or get her mad at me, or something, but she knows what Southie was, okay? The forced busing and everything else, and she knows that that's not who I am. I've been very honest with her.

MARGARET

He told you that fight story?

KATE

No, not *that* story. That story's pretty shitty.

MIKE

It's not like she said, Katie.

MARGARET

And did he mention we used to date?

(Silence.)

MIKE

What are you doing?

MARGARET

What, you said you were honest with each other.

KATE

You dated?

MIKE

Just for like a month.

MARGARET

Two months.

MIKE

Two months. In high school. Over the summer.

KATE

Okay.

MARGARET

See, she's fine with that. *(To Kate)* He told me not to mention it, so—

MIKE

That's not true.

169

KATE

You told her not to mention it?

MIKE

No, that's / not—

MARGARET

Yes you did. You said to keep it secret.

MIKE

Margaret—

MARGARET

That's what you said. Or maybe it's just what I *heard*.

MIKE

Okay.

MARGARET

You said to not mention it because she might get weird.

MIKE

Why are doing this? Because I won't let you babysit?

KATE

Why would I get weird?

MIKE

Look, I didn't tell you because it's not how— I don't even think of Margaret like that, as an ex— We were friends for so long. I just think of her as a friend.

KATE

So what's the big deal?

MIKE

There is none.

KATE

Then why not mention you dated?

MIKE

Because you're sensitive about that stuff, for obvious reasons, and
I didn't want to rock the boat.

KATE

So you thought lying to me was better?

MIKE

I didn't lie. I just didn't . . .

KATE

Tell the truth?

MIKE

Kate—

KATE

Are we actually having this conversation again?

MIKE

No, I— Can we / not—

KATE

And you wonder why I don't wanna stop seeing / the counselor.

MIKE

I said I'd see her! I was just asking whether we— *(Turns on Margaret)*
Why did you come here! I told you there was no party!

MARGARET

Why are you getting angry?

MIKE

I've tried to be nice to you, Margaret.

MARGARET

You *have* been nice.

MIKE

I tried to be a good sport, even though I haven't seen you in thirty
years. I don't really know you, but I invite you out here . . .

MARGARET

Oh, you don't know me?

MIKE

Not anymore, no. Neither of us know each other. And I'm sorry
if / that—

MARGARET

You don't know me. / Okay.

MIKE

That's what happens! When you don't see each / other for—

MARGARET

You *asked* me to come out here, by the way, so don't make it seem /
like I—

MIKE

You obviously turned into some kind of a troublemaker, / or—

MARGARET

Is that what I am?

MIKE

Yeah, you don't get your way so you have this tantrum.

MARGARET

What tantrum? Who's having a tantrum?

MIKE

Not literally! A figurative tantrum! Stop being so simpleminded!

MARGARET   KATE
Wow.   Michael—

MIKE

I don't return your calls, so you push your way into my office!

MARGARET

I'm simpleminded now.

MIKE

I don't let you babysit, so you start stirring the shit. You're *punishing* me for not giving you what you want.

KATE

Okay, Michael.

MIKE

But *I'm* the asshole. Because I don't want a stranger watching my kid. Because I have a nice house. Because I buy my wife gifts. That makes me an asshole.

MARGARET

No, that makes you lace-curtain.

MIKE

You know what? I think we should probably call it a night. Because you are really starting to piss me off.

MARGARET

You kicking me out, Mikey?

MIKE

(To Kate) Can you get her coat, please?

MARGARET

You're kicking me out.

KATE

Nobody's kicking anyone out. Margaret— Michael, relax.

MIKE

You wanna take some of the cheese, Margie? Kate can bag it up if you like it.

MARGARET

I didn't even want to come here. *You* invited *me.*

MIKE

No, you kinda invited yourself!

KATE

Would you—

MARGARET

I only came here because I needed a job.

MIKE

Well it's not my fault you can't find one!

KATE

Ally's asleep.

MIKE

I'm sorry that you made some bad choices in your life, but that is not / my fault.

MARGARET

Oh, I had choices?

MIKE

Yeah. And if thinking you *didn't* makes your life a little more bearable, that's fine. But it isn't true.

MARGARET

What choices did I have?

MIKE

All the way back. The things you did, the people you hung out with.

MARGARET

The people I—? We hung out with the *same* people!

MIKE

Plus you never applied yourself. Not at school or / anywhere else.

MARGARET

I didn't have someone checking my homework like you did, Mikey. My mother was too busy killing herself at that box factory.

MIKE

Oh poor you.

MARGARET

And you're right, I *did* drop out of school. Was that a choice though?

MIKE

Of course it was. Girls have babies, and still stay in school.

KATE

Are you serious?

175

MIKE

They *do*!

MARGARET

Well I chose to take care of the baby instead. Because that's what people did. I got a job. I got a bunch of jobs in fact. And every one of them sucked, because what other job *could* I get? Not much of a choice there either, I'm afraid.

MIKE

And you lost most of those jobs?

MARGARET

As a matter of fact, I did.

MIKE

Why?

MARGARET

Usually because I was late.

MIKE

Well there's a choice.

KATE

Would you stop it?

MIKE

What, she chose to be late.

MARGARET

I didn't *choose* to be late. Shit happened, that *made* me late! Sometimes it was Joyce. Sometimes it was the T.

KATE

You don't have to explain / yourself to him.

176

MARGARET

One time I got my car taken. Why'd I lose the car? Because I missed a payment. Why'd I miss a payment? Because I had to pay for a dentist instead. Why'd I have to pay the dentist?

MIKE

We don't need the / sob story—

MARGARET

No, I've done this a hundred times in my head, Mikey. I think you should hear it, too. Why'd I have to pay the dentist? Because I didn't have insurance, and I cracked a tooth and ignored it for six months, until an abscess formed. Why'd I crack a tooth?

MIKE

I don't /care!

MARGARET

Because one night I thought I'd save a little money, and skip dinner! But I got hungry and decided to snack on a piece of candy brittle. And that's all it took—a piece of fucking candy brittle, and I was out of a job again.

And that's how it always is. And if it's not the candy brittle then it's Joyce's medication, or my phone getting cut off, or Russell Gillis breaking in and stealing my goddamn microwave! And you wanna tell me about choices? While you sit up here practically breaking your arm patting yourself on the back for all you accomplished. Lucky you. You made some wise choices. But you're wrong if you think everyone has 'em.

In fact, the only *real* choice I ever *did* make was dumping you. And yeah, I've thought about it a million times since: "What woulda happened if I hadn't dumped Mikey Dillon?" Maybe I wouldn't have ended up with Gobie, or maybe I woulda finished school, or maybe this coulda been *my* house.

177

(Silence. They look at her, confused.)

Maybe it coulda been. All of this. Maybe it coulda been mine.

MIKE

Jesus, Margie, what does that even mean? We dated for *two months!*

KATE

Be nice.

MIKE

(To Kate) Two months! And you heard her, *she* dumped *me! (Back to Margaret)* Which you didn't seem all that upset about at the time. You were with Gobie like three days later.

MARGARET

And why do you think that was?

MIKE

Because I didn't mean anything to you!

MARGARET

Wrong!

MIKE

Honestly, you've made up this thing in your head!

MARGARET

Joyce wasn't premature.

(Silence. Kate looks from Margaret to Mike.)

KATE

What does that mean?

MIKE

What are you doing, Margie?

KATE

What does that mean? "Joyce wasn't premature."

MARGARET

Don't say you didn't have help getting out of Southie. You had help. And not just your dad. If I hadn't let you go, you'd still be there right now.

MIKE

If you hadn't let / me go?

MARGARET

You'd be working down at the variety store with Johnny Dugger. I let you go.

MIKE

All right, Margaret. I knew you were having trouble, but I didn't realize you were pathological.

MARGARET

Joyce didn't have all those problems because she came early, she just had those problems. She was full-term. Late, in fact. I just said she was premature so Gobie would think she / was his.

MIKE

You *know* this is bullshit, Katie.

KATE

No I don't.

MARGARET

(To Kate) I'm sorry. I wasn't gonna say anything but—

179

MIKE

Was this the idea? You thought you'd come here / and—

MARGARET

I could've kept you there, that's all I'm saying. If I wanted to.

MIKE

How'd you come up with this? Were you watchin' *General Hospital* one day and think, oh, here's an angle.

MARGARET

You wanna do a blood test?

KATE

What the fuck, / Michael?

MIKE

No, I don't want to do a blood test, because that is not my / child!

MARGARET

Why would I lie?

MIKE

Why? To squeeze me for money! To pay your rent! To do everything that you can't get Gobie to do! There's a hundred reasons / for you to lie!

MARGARET

I could've trapped you. That's what girls did, you know. They'd get pregnant to trap guys.

MIKE

Is that what you're trying to do now? Because you're a little late.

MARGARET

I didn't do that to you. But I *could've*. I let you go.

MIKE

And why would you do that?

MARGARET

Because you were going off to college! Because I didn't want to be the thing that ruined your life! BECAUSE I WAS NICE!

MIKE

Oh yeah, you're a sweetheart. Shoving your way in here, making up these bullshit / stories—

MARGARET

They're not bull / shit.

MIKE

You know what, Margie? It wouldn't have mattered. Even if any of this were true, which it isn't, it still wouldn't have mattered. You didn't do me any favors breaking up with me. I was gonna do it myself, but you beat me to it. You think I wanted a girlfriend when I was heading off to *college*? Do you know how many women were *at* U-Penn? We wouldn't have stayed together. Baby or no baby. I wouldn't have stayed.

MARGARET

Don't say that.

MIKE

I wouldn't have. No way. I'm sorry. I would've taken off anyway.

MARGARET

No you wouldn't have. That's not who you were.

MIKE

Are you kidding? I knew Southie was a black hole before I was thirteen. I wouldn't have stayed there for anything. Not for *you*. No way. Not for some retarded baby.

KATE

Jesus, Michael.

MIKE

I'm sorry. But self-preservation. I would've been one of those deadbeats that take off. Just like your father took off. Just like Gobie took off. That would've been me.

MARGARET

You're just saying that.

MIKE

Why?

MARGARET

I don't know why, but I don't believe you.

MIKE

(Lunging at her) AND I DON'T BELIEVE *YOU!*

KATE

(Blocking his way) STOP IT, MICHAEL!

(Silence.)

MARGARET

There he is. There's still a little Southie in there.

MIKE

Too far, Margie. I know you're desperate but this is too far.

MARGARET

(After a beat, more to herself) You were gonna dump me anyway. *(Beat)* That's a mean thing to say, Mikey.

MIKE

Why?

MARGARET

Because it means that nothing woulda been different. That there really *was* nothing I coulda done to get outta there. *(Beat)* It's a pretty fucking depressing thought. That's why.

(Margaret gets her coat on.)

(To Kate as she goes) I'm sorry, I didn't mean to— I shouldn't have / come here.

KATE

(Stops her) Why didn't you come find him earlier? *(Beat)* If the baby stuff is true—

MARGARET

It *is* true.

KATE

Then why didn't you come find him?

MARGARET

I told you. Because . . . I didn't want— Because . . .

KATE

Because it was the nice thing to do. To let him go.

MARGARET

Yeah.

KATE

(Beat) But that doesn't sound nice to me. Not for your daughter, at least.

MARGARET

My daughter?

KATE

You talk about how hard it's been and how you've struggled with her all these years—

MARGARET

I *have*.

KATE

Why? If you didn't have to struggle, why *would* you? Because you didn't want to inconvenience Mike?

MARGARET

No, that's / not—

KATE

I'd do anything for my daughter. If there was / something—

MARGARET

So would I.

KATE

Then your story doesn't make any *sense*.

MARGARET

No of course not. You gotta stand by your man, so—

KATE

No, I don't actually.

MARGARET

Well I don't know what to tell ya.

KATE

You could've looked him up at any point, and said, "Hey, I know this sucks, but I could really use your help with our kid." That's what *I* would've done.

MARGARET

Well I'm not you.

KATE

That's right. You're not. *(Beat)* I could never put my pride ahead of my daughter.

MARGARET

Hey, take it easy.

KATE

And I *have* had to make that choice. Haven't I, Michael?

MIKE

Kate, enough.

KATE

A *few* times. And my pride always lost. My daughter's more important.

MARGARET

You think mine's not?

KATE

Not if your story's true. Because if it is, you're saying you let her suffer needlessly.

MARGARET

That is not what I'm saying.

KATE

Isn't it?

MARGARET

(Beat) No.

KATE

Yes it is, Margaret. Which I could understand if you said, well I was scared, or stubborn, or I didn't know how to get out of the situation, or I couldn't be / bothered to—

MARGARET

Which is all true!

KATE

But that's not what you said! You said you did it because you're a nice person! Which, I'm sorry, is a *stretch*. Especially when you start pitting me and Michael against each other. When you already know we're having trouble.

MARGARET

I don't know anything about / that.

KATE

Yes, you do! Jesus, *everyone* knows! Ya spend five minutes with us / and—

MIKE

That's not / true.

KATE

Not now, Michael. *(Back to Margaret)* The point is, you knew what you were doing. And I'm sorry this isn't your life, Margaret, but that's not *my* fault. And it's not Ally's fault. We didn't do anything to you.

MARGARET

Of course not.

KATE

This is *our* life. And I'm not gonna let you come in here and deliberately try to sabotage us. That is just spite.

MARGARET

That's not what I was doing.

KATE

Well it's what you did. And I don't know if any of the other stuff is true or not, but I can tell you one thing—you are not nice. You are *not*. *(Beat) Is* it true, by the way? The stuff about your daughter? Because if it is, Michael will just have to man up / and provide.

MIKE

Katie, stop.

KATE

We'll write you a check right now. If it's true. *(Beat)* Is it, Margaret?

MARGARET

(After a pause) I *told* her it was stupid. Jeannie. I told her it was a stupid idea. "Just say Joyce wasn't premature." She thought it'd be funny. *(Beat)* You're right, it wasn't nice. *(To Mike)* But you pissed me off with that babysitting thing. You could've let me watch her, Mike. It wouldn't have been any skin off your nose.

MIKE

You see, Katie? She made it up.

MARGARET

I'm sorry.

MIKE

People go to jail for this kinda thing, you know. What you just did?

MARGARET

You gonna call the cops, Mikey?

MIKE

(To Kate) And she wants to say she doesn't make choices.

MARGARET

I'm gonna go.

MIKE

(Grabs the flowerpot rabbit) Take this too, wouldja?

MARGARET

That was a gift.

MIKE

I don't want it.

MARGARET

Come on, it's a *gift*.

MIKE

And every time I look at it, I'm gonna think about what you just pulled. Take the rabbit.

MARGARET

It's for your daughter.

MIKE

Margaret—

MARGARET

I don't want it.

(Mike hurls it against a wall. It smashes to pieces.)

MARGARET	KATE
Hey!	Jesus, Michael!

MARGARET

I paid for that.

MIKE

(A little laugh) Okay.

MARGARET

I PAID FOR IT!

(He shrugs. Margaret, seething, rushes to the crystal vase.)

KATE AND MIKE

No-no-no-no-no-no!

(She's about to throw it to the floor, but she stops.)

MARGARET

What's the point? *(Hands it to Mike)* It's *insured.*

VOICE OF ALLY

Dad? . . . Daddy?

KATE

It's okay, honey. Daddy just dropped something. I'll be right up.

*(Kate heads up the stairs.
    Margaret and Mike are silent for a few moments.)*

189

MIKE

Are you all right?

MARGARET

(A wry chuckle) Am I all right.

MIKE

What'd you think was gonna happen, Margie?

MARGARET

I don't know. I just wanted a job. That's all. I just wanted a job.

MIKE

You can't blame me for your life, you know.

MARGARET

I don't. I just think you got lucky. That's all I was trying to say.

MIKE

I wouldn't call it luck, but okay.

MARGARET

What if your father hadn't come out to stop that fight with the black kid? *(Beat)* You would've killed that boy.

MIKE

No, that . . . You make too much out of everything. It never got close to that.

MARGARET

Yes it did. You know it did. You could be sitting up in Walpole right now, bunkin' with Marty McDermott.

MIKE

That wouldn't have happened.

MARGARET

If your father wasn't watching from the kitchen window it would've.

MIKE

But he *was*.

MARGARET

Which is *lucky*, that's all I'm saying. I never had anyone watching from a window for me. You got lucky. One hiccup, and it could've been *you* looking for work instead of me. Or you dying up on that sidewalk instead of Cookie. That could just as easily have been you, Mikey.

MIKE

I don't think so.

MARGARET

No?

MIKE

No.

MARGARET

(Beat. Referring to the house) Then all this is wasted on you. *(Beat)* And it wasn't my job to come looking for you, by the way. Not when you knew. You should tell that to your wife.

MIKE

Are you actually starting / that again?

MARGARET

And if you didn't know, you must've suspected at least, that she *could've* been yours. *That* at least. The thought must've crossed your mind. *(Beat)* Did it?

(Silence. He just stares at her.)

It wasn't my job to find you. Not when you knew where we were.

MIKE

Margaret—

MARGARET

And there was no way I was gonna beg. I can get damn close. Obviously. But I won't beg. Not even for Joyce. And if that makes me a bad mother, then I guess I'm a bad mother.

MIKE

You're not.

MARGARET

I know I'm not.

(Kate comes down the stairs and back into the living room.)

KATE

She wants her dad.

MIKE

All right.

MARGARET

Sorry we woke her up.

KATE

That's okay. I'm more upset about the rabbit actually. I think she would've really liked it.

MIKE

I'm gonna go up and see her.

MARGARET

I was just about to head out anyway.

KATE

I'm sorry, can you just—

(Mike and Margaret both stop.)

You *were* lying, right? About your daughter?

MARGARET

(Beat) Yeah, I was lying.

KATE

(Beat) Okay.

MARGARET

(Beat) I *do* think he's fucking that Dominican receptionist though.

(Kate and Mike stare at her.)

Just kidding.

(Then she turns, heads out through the foyer, and out the front door. Lights out.)

Scene 2

Church basement. Margaret, Jean, Dottie and Stevie are at their folding table playing bingo. We hear the voice of the priest, and the murmur of the crowd. The women are mid-conversation.

JEAN

(To Margaret) Why didn't you tell me? I gotta hear it from Dottie of all people?

DOTTIE

What's that mean?

JEAN

(Still to Margaret) Finally some good news.

MARGARET

It's not good news.

DOTTIE

Of course it is.

MARGARET

It's no news. It's nothing.

DOTTIE

You're nuts.

JEAN

It came in the mail?

DOTTIE

It came in the mail. A stack of bills, with a note: "Margaret's rent."

MARGARET

That's not my rent, Dottie.

DOTTIE

Hell it ain't. It said right on it: "Margaret's rent." Can't get much clearer than that.

MARGARET

I'm gonna mail it back to him.

DOTTIE

No you're not. Not *this* money. You find it somewhere else, 'cause that money is ear-marked.

VOICE OF PRIEST

First up is B-12.

JEAN

Just take it and forget it.

VOICE OF PRIEST

B . . . 12.

DOTTIE

You're lucky, Margie. My Russell was all set to move in. I told him I couldn't do that to you. I told him I wanted to give you a little more time. Good thing that envelope arrived when it did. Ya made it in under the wire. I said, sorry Russell, there's no room at the inn.

VOICE OF PRIEST

N-33.

DOTTIE

Which is lucky. I would've missed Joyce.

VOICE OF PRIEST

N . . . 33.

JEAN

(To Margaret) Did Mikey say he was gonna send money?

MARGARET

No.

JEAN

Did you *ask* for it?

MARGARET

No, Jean, of *course* not. Did I *ask* for it?

STEVIE

Maybe he just wanted to help out.

MARGARET

Yeah, I don't think so.

STEVIE

Why not?

MARGARET

It's not in his nature.

DOTTIE

Of course it is. Why else would he send that envelope?

MARGARET

It doesn't matter, I'm not taking it.

VOICE OF PRIEST

I-22.

DOTTIE

She goes there looking for money, then she gets all proud when she *gets* it.

VOICE OF PRIEST

I . . . 22.

MARGARET

I went looking for a job, not a handout.

DOTTIE

Tomato-tomahto.

JEAN

What'd you say to him?

MARGARET

Nothing.

JEAN

And he just pays your rent?

MARGARET

He's not paying my rent.

DOTTIE

He already has.

VOICE OF PRIEST

O-61.

JEAN

Maybe the wife sent it.

VOICE OF PRIEST

O . . . 61.

JEAN

You think the wife sent it?

MARGARET

I don't know. I don't care. I'm sending it back.

JEAN

I swear to god, Margaret, the first break you've gotten since I've known you, and you want to toss it back in. It's not like you don't deserve it.

MARGARET

I don't want that money.

DOTTIE

It's already been deposited.

MARGARET

What are you talking about? It's not your money to deposit, / Dottie.

DOTTIE

The envelope was / addressed to *me*!

JEAN

You're being awful hardheaded, / Marg—

MARGARET

I'm not taking his money.

STEVIE

Jesus! It's not his money!

(Silence. He looks up at them.)

He didn't send the money. And neither did the wife.

MARGARET

(Beat) Stevie . . .

STEVIE

You make everything so difficult, you know it? Don't you know what a gift horse is?

MARGARET

I assumed Mike sent it.

STEVIE

Well he didn't.

MARGARET

You don't have money to be paying my rent.

STEVIE

I won last week. It wasn't much, but it was enough. And I never win at bingo.

MARGARET

Stevie—

STEVIE

You needed it more than I did.

MARGARET

Still, you can't—

STEVIE

Can you stop? You'll pay me back when you can.

(Pause.)

MARGARET

Okay.

VOICE OF PRIEST

B-5. B . . . 5.

MARGARET

Thank you.

STEVIE

You're welcome.

DOTTIE

(After a few beats) So what are you gonna do *next* month?

(Beat. Jean slowly turns to her.)

JEAN

What is wrong with you?

DOTTIE

What. It's a logical question.

VOICE OF PRIEST

G-51. G . . . 51.

JEAN

You didn't mention Joyce?

MARGARET

No, I did. He didn't believe she was his. *(Beat)* I always thought you didn't know about that.

JEAN

(Looks at her) Everybody knew.

VOICE OF PRIEST

N-43. N . . . 43.

DOTTIE

Did he like my rabbit, Margie?

MARGARET

He threw it against a wall.

DOTTIE

(Beat. Confused) Well why would he do that?

VOICE OF PRIEST

O-72. O . . . 72.

MARGARET

I'll try Gillette this week. See if I can get something down there. Can you call your brother, Stevie? See if he can get me in there?

STEVIE

(Beat) Sure. I'll talk to him.

MARGARET

Thanks.

JEAN

It's something at least.

MARGARET

Yeah, it's something.

JEAN

And if not Gillette, then something else.

MARGARET

Yup.

JEAN

Something'll come up.

MARGARET

I hope so.

VOICE OF PRIEST

G-53.

(Bingo daubers raised, they scan their cards searching for the number. Nothing.)

G . . . 53.

(They continue to search their cards as the lights slowly fade.)

END OF PLAY

DAVID LINDSAY-ABAIRE is a play-wright, screenwriter, lyricist and librettist, whose play *Rabbit Hole* premiered on Broadway, and went on to receive the 2007 Pulitzer Prize for Drama, the Spirit of America Award, and five Tony nominations (including Best Play). His previous play *Kimberly Akimbo* was commissioned by South Coast Repertory Theatre, premiered at that theater, and received the L.A. Drama Critics Circle Award for play-writing, three Garland Awards and the Kesselring Prize. The play went on to a sold-out New York run at Manhattan Theatre Club (MTC), where it was hailed as "The Comedy of the Year" by the *New York Times*. David's play *Wonder of the World* premiered at Washington, D.C.'s Woolly Mammoth Theatre Company, where it was nominated for a Helen Hayes Award as Outstanding New Play of the Year, and also went on to a sold-out New York run at MTC. His play *Fuddy Meers* premiered at MTC in the fall of 1999, and later transferred to The Minetta Lane Theatre for a commercial run. *Fuddy* has since received more than five hundred productions around the country and abroad, including London's West End. David was most recently nominated for a Grammy Award with Composer Jeanine Tesori (Best Musical Show Album)

JOAN MARCUS

and two Tony Awards (Best Book of a Musical, and Best Score) for their work on *Shrek the Musical*. Prior to that, David was awarded the 2008 Ed Kleban Award as America's most promising musical-theater lyricist. In addition to his work in theater, David's film credits include his screen adaptation of *Rabbit Hole* (Academy Award–nomination for Nicole Kidman), as well as the upcoming features *Rise of the Guardians* (Dreamworks) and *Oz: The Great and Powerful* (Disney). David is a proud New Dramatists alum, a graduate of Sarah Lawrence College and the Juilliard School, as well as a member of the Writers Guild of America and The Dramatists Guild Council.